MIKE'S EYE ON THE ISLAND

A Quizzical Chronicle of Life In Palm Beach and Beyond

by Michael I. Price

PALM BEACH   FLORIDA   2005

Published by Red Sneaker Publishing
A Subsidiary of Michael I. Price, Inc.

http:/www.michaelpricephotography.com

The stories in this book originally appeared in
The Palm Beach Daily News
Palm Beach, Florida
2003-2005

ISBN 0-9771751-0-3

Cover Design by Jeff Lewis/Cobalt Design Studio
West Palm Beach, Florida

Manufactured in the United States of America
First Edition

For additional copies or information contact:
Michael Price, 500 Marlin Road, North Palm Beach, FL. 33408
pricephoto@bellsouth.net

Printed in the United States by Morris Publishing
3212 East Highway 30
Kearney, NE 68847
1-800-650-7888

The creation of these stories could not have been possible if not for the adventures of my family and friends. I am also deeply indebted to my editors Deborah and Lou, who have exercised unrelenting support and great grammatical judgment. Of course I would be remiss not to acknowledge Joyce Reingold, publisher, and Pat Thomas, editor, of The Palm Beach Daily News, who have given me the opportuity each week to share my tales.

CONTENTS

'DOWN & OUT' IN PALM BEACH

I've been called a lot of things in my lifetime, but I heard a new one recently - "homeless guy." Even more remarkable, I heard it twice in as many days.

In both instances, an acquaintance walked by me on Worth Avenue, turned around and said, "Hello Michael, I thought you were a homeless guy sitting there." All I could muster as a sarcastic response was "Thanks." Ever since those incidences I've been racking my brain on just what would constitute a "homeless-looking guy" in Palm Beach.

First off, each day I was wearing a Ralph Lauren Polo Shirt, Gap khaki shorts, my trademark red Saucony sneakers and my Costa del Mar polarized sunglasses. And I was cleanly shaven. Next to me was a folding handcart (not a shopping cart) stacked neatly with three matching black canvas bags containing lighting equipment, a digital camera with various lenses and lastly a Dell Inspirion 8500 Computer. All totaled, enough to pay for the sales tax on a Mercedes Maybach.

I didn't think I fit the profile, but maybe Palm Beach has different standards than the rest of the country. To be sure I called Janet Kinsella, media spokeswoman at the Palm Beach Police Department. "Janet, do I fit the stereotype for a homeless guy in Palm Beach?" "Actually we don't have a profile for a homeless person" was her answer. In that case, I guess I could be mistaken for a homeless guy (and so could Ron Perelman). I needed one more opinion to be sure.

John Surovek, former president of the Worth Avenue Association and gallery owner in Via Parigi for more than 25 years, weighed in with his view on the matter. "I wouldn't think anyone would mistake you for homeless. Homely, maybe."

Thankfully, I'm gainfully employed and live in a comfortable abode in North Palm Beach. My wife constantly reminds me that we are truly fortunate and if I were more spiritual, even blessed. Then I think about those stories in the Palm Beach Post about a family of six living in the back of a station wagon; people who are really homeless.

I still didn't have an answer to my question, but if one more person makes that same mistake I will personally berate them into making a donation to The Salvation Army, Home Safe or any one of the many other organizations that help the homeless. Now if you mistake me for George Clooney or Brad Pitt, that's another situation entirely.

LA RONDA: A CONCRETE CHOICE

La Ronda, which in Hungarian means "house that sticks out like a sore thumb," is an architectural masterpiece. My credentials? I loved watching The Jetsons and spent a portion of my childhood living amid the decaying deco of Miami Beach.

Unfortunately the great white mammoth on North Lake Way is destined for the big dumpster in the sky, and understandably there are a few preservationists very upset. And one happens to be Jane Volk, widow of the architect John Volk who designed the home. Absent of landmark status, there was little she or anyone else could do to save the home I've been infatuated with for almost 30 years.

My one opportunity to set foot in La Ronda came a year after it was first placed on the market following the deaths of its owners. I called the listing broker, Lawrence Moens, and persuaded him to let me use the home for a fashion shoot. It would be good publicity for the marketing of the home and at the same time offer great backgrounds for my photos.

Upon walking into the cavernous living room, my first impression was that the style was more outdated than outlandish. I had deja vu of the 1964 World's Fair, and felt there was a bunch of schoolchildren around me singing "It's a Small World After All". I think I also felt car sick.

Snapping myself back into the here and now, I tried to gaze out over the pool, past the lake and onward toward the main entrance of Good Samaritan Medical Center. But I couldn't see a thing because there was so much concrete reflecting light around that I needed two pairs of polarized sunglasses just to open the glass sliders. The last time I saw so much concrete was when I drove over the Hoover Dam.

Granted, my expertise in interior design is thumbing through Architectural Digest once every few months, but I couldn't imagine how anyone could transform this "dinosaur" into a livable, usable space. OK, maybe just one person - my friend Bruce Helander.

So it came as no surprise when I heard the new owners wanted to tear the house down and replace it with a much more "sensible" home. Like so many other pieces of Florida's short history, this one too will be lost. I'll miss seeing the familiar elliptical roof line from North Flagler Drive, but then again, maybe I'll be better off paying attention to the traffic while I talk on my cell phone.

LET'S MAKE A DEAL

I thought I had seen it all - that is, until I got a certain letter in the mail.

Five years ago, my wife's decade-old car bit the dust and we needed to replace it before she headed off to work the following day. Glancing at the full-page automotive ads in the paper, one in particular jumped out at me: A brand new Japanese import. I got out a magnifying glass and read over the fine, fine, fine print. Yes indeed, that was the price; the only additional costs were for the tax and tag, and yes, the steering wheel and floor mats were included.

I cut out the advertisement and went over to the dealership. I was greeted by a man with a magnanimous smile and beautiful Caribbean lilt in his voice. This was Colin Dunbar. (Names have been changed for the sake of privacy.) Before the sales pitch could start, I held out the newspaper ad and said, "I want this car at this price." His reply was, "No problem, mon." A half-hour later we drove away in our brand new car.

It's been five years of trouble-free driving and we've had no reason to return the car to the dealership until recently, for a minor recall to replace an electrical part. While waiting for the work to be done I noticed my salesman, Colin, in the showroom. I was surprised to see him as the turnover rate in the car business is notorious. We spoke for a few minutes and I left by telling him how pleasurable it was to buy a car from him.

Last week I got a letter from the car dealership. It stated, "Dear Mr. Price, It is with a heavy heart that we write to you to inform you that your sales representative, Mr. Colin Dunbar, passed away on September 20th . . ." The letter went on to state that Colin had been a dedicated employee for more than 10 years and was respected and admired by all his fellow employees and friends. I could see why.

Now here is the kicker. The letter's last paragraph began, "Since you are a valued client here we want to introduce you to another of our sales representatives, Mr. Jim Nelson. If you have any questions or concerns about your vehicle or need any assistance with a new one, please call Jim directly." I'm not sure if it was the garlic-infused sardine burrito I had for lunch, but I was beginning to get a bad taste in my mouth.

I'm all for those wacky balloons and colossal American flags, and sometimes I can even tolerate those horrible radio ads, but this was too much.

Margaret Wilesmith, president of Wilesmith Advertising and Design in West Palm Beach, agreed with me. "What you have here is the classic bad news/good news campaign. The bad news is your sales associate has passed away, the good news is we have another person who can sell you a new car. The least they could have done was send two letters a month apart, one imparting the bad news, the second one introducing another associate. There is no low to which a car dealer will not stoop."

She said it, not me.

THE REAL DOPE ON
C.Z. GUEST WAS ME

I'm sure C.Z. Guest didn't remember the day we met, but there were plenty of others who do.

Back in the the winter of 1986 I was not only the rookie photographer at the Shiny Sheet, but the unofficial Employee Parking Lot Monitor, as well. The newsroom was a precursor to Starbucks. People stopped by with their pets, pastries, coffee. They would want to chat away the morning, or try to get a few bits of gossip, and we were all too happy to indulge and eat the doughnuts.

And therein lay the problem. The parking lot was designed to accommodate 15 cars, and at times there would be 30 or more vehicles packed in. Being administrator material, I implemented a plan to allow the photography department to use the spaces closest to the parking lot exit in the event we had to make a mad dash to a DAR or a Rotary Club luncheon. Breaking news breaks fast, and we wanted to be the first out the door and the first to take a bite of the lobster salad.

One balmy December morning a reporter rushed into the photo department and told me that I needed to get over to The Breakers pronto. I'm thinking Chamber of Commerce breakfast - fresh-squeezed orange juice with a cheese Danish. But no, a bale of marijuana had just washed up on the beach, and we needed a photograph of it.

Not one to miss a Pulitzer Prize opportunity, I rushed out to the parking lot only to discover I was blocked in by a white Jeep Wagoneer. I ran back into the newsroom and yelled, "Whoever owns that white Jeep better move it now!" The chatter came to a screeching halt and all eyes were on me.

I noticed a woman wearing khaki capri pants, white oxford button-down shirt with a strand of pearls around her neck sitting on the corner of a desk, the publisher standing alongside her. I heard someone in the room say, "That's C.Z. Guest's Jeep." And of course I said, "I don't care who C.Z.'s guest is, there is a bale of dope on the beach, and I need to get my car out of the lot now!"

I can't deny that it was me who felt like the dope that morning back in 1986, but maybe C.Z. was talking with Truman Capote later that day and mentioned a funny thing that happened to her while at the Palm Beach Daily News. For me, it was just another one of those days that I haven't forgotten.

7

WHAT ARE FRIENDS FOR?

There I was at Cucina having breakfast with Rod Stewart and his girlfriend Penny (actually, they were sitting at the table next to me) when I began to wonder how long it would be before someone interrupted my omelette in mid-bite to ask me for an autograph, or tell me how much they enjoyed looking at my last photograph. Thankfully neither of us were disturbed that morning, which is one of the great advantages of Palm Beach . . . the more famous you are, the less people care about you.

I was once queried by a People magazine scribe about my good friend and former Palm Beach resident John Lennon (actually, I was eavesdropping on photographer Lucien Capehart's interview). Capehart told him, "John liked Palm Beach because everyone here left him alone. They were either too rich or too old to pay any attention to him." Well, I guess that's one explanation.

When I was invited to Celine Dion's house for dinner (actually, I was there photographing her dining room table for a furniture maker), I realized that celebrities are really no different from the rest of us, except they have nicer bathroom fixtures.

I remember spending an afternoon on South Beach with actress Christina Applegate (actually, it was Key Biscayne, and I was there doing still photos for a commercial she was filming), when I realized we had both ordered the same exact meal for lunch. Of course, it was only a coincidence that she too would have noted had she looked out the window of the air-conditioned Winnebago and seen me sitting in the blistering sun with 80 members of the film crew.

Prince Philip and I were chatting for a few moments together, catching up on old times (actually, he was telling me how inept I was as a photographer because I needed to take more than one picture of him and his guests) when it occurred to me what a royal pain in the arse he really is. I said, "Phil, I'm out of here. Cheerio." I haven't heard a word from him since.

Dan Marino invited me over to his house for drinks one summer afternoon (actually, I was there taking a portrait of his wife, Claire, and she offered me a glass of water) when I couldn't help but ask if Dan would mind me rummaging through his closet (actually, I asked his wife if I could go pick out a clean football jersey for the photo shoot).

There I was in Dan Marino's closet surrounded by Armani suits. I think I heard Dan say, "Mi casa es su casa" before I left.

Burt Reynolds and I never got along. When ex-wife Loni Anderson came crying on my shoulder (actually, she just brushed my shoulder while walking past me in the airport) I knew that Burt's threat to "rip my head off" wasn't to be taken lightly (see the Palm Beach Law Review Vol. 35 No. 187). Although, I do believe Burt has been doing a great job in those Maaco commercials.

I once spent an afternoon hanging around with Paul Newman at the Daytona International Speedway (actually, I spent the afternoon hanging around waiting for Paul Newman). I'll never forget when Paul asked the security guard, "Is this guy with us?" What a joker that Paul! "Of course I'm with you, Paul," I said. "I've watched Cool Hand Luke more than 30 times."

Now I'm telling you from personal experience that Jack Nicholson is a real piece of work. I was in a hotel suite (actually, I was in a hotel room with Rebecca Broussard, one of his ex-girlfriends and mother of two of his children, and her friend, actress Joan Cusack, during an interview session) when Broussard told me she had to leave the room "to make a private call" to Jack back in Los Angeles. I took this to be a cry for help, and sure enough, they broke up a few years later.

One of the film industry's most respected actors and my close personal friend Michael Caine (actually, we both share the same first name and have the letter C in our last names) once asked me to meet him "under the bridge" at the Intracoastal Waterway in Fort Lauderdale. I wondered, why the cloak-and-danger stuff? Was this connected to the run-in with the Royal Family? It just so happened he was staying at a hotel next to the bridge and his publicist couldn't give me better directions. Before I left, I gave Mike a present - a streetmap of South Florida. Now that's what you call a gift that keeps on giving.

When Oprah and I were working out together at the Doral Spa (actually, she was there lifting weights, I was there lifting liquid spirits) I couldn't help but suggest to her that takeout from Shula's Steakhouse wasn't the way to go, even though Don Shula is a close personal friend (actually, I once sat across the table from him during a press conference). When I saw her recently on the cover of the National Enquirer, she looked as though she had taken my advice. That's what friends are for.

I'm really feeling sorry for my close personal friend Rush Limbaugh. (Actually, I only listened to his radio show once, but met his wife in person). I had back problems, too, and suggested he try yoga. He didn't listen. That must have been when he had hearing problems. I first met my good friend Gwyneth Paltrow at Cafe L'Europe (actually, she was there with her grandmother, but we had the same waiter). Initially I didn't recognize her, but then overheard Gwyneth asking the waiter, "Is that Michael Price sitting at that table over there?" So much for a quiet dinner.

A few weeks ago, I was hanging around The Breakers Beach Club with my fishing buddy Jimmy Buffett (actually, I was taking his photo at a charity event) when it occurred to me how obnoxious people are who "name drop." No sooner was I about to say this to Jimmy, but guess who comes strolling in? My old friend Matt Lauer! (actually, I catch 'Today' whenever I can.) Now I'm sitting there with Jimmy and Matt, and I say, "Have I ever told you two about the time I was invited to meet Pope John Paul II and President Ronald Reagan at Miami International Airport ?"

OUT TO LUNCH WITH MORT KAYE

I wouldn't label myself a procrastinator, but when Mort Kaye invited me to join him for lunch in 1986 I didn't think it would be 17 years before we got to order our food.

When I remind Mort of our long-overdue luncheon, I suggest somewhere informal like Testa's or Toojay's, but Mort's reply is, "How does Cafe Boulud sound to you?" French and expensive comes to my mind. Then the classic Mort Kaye: "Don't worry, it's my treat."

So I'm sitting at a table at Cafe Boulud waiting for Mort and pondering the fact that I've known him for almost two decades. There have been days when I've crossed paths with him three or four times, but I can't recall having a conversation with him that lasted more than two or three minutes. What I know about him comes from anecdotes other people have told me, possibly a bit exaggerated.

Three years ago, I, along with film producer and former Palm Beacher Francine Bernard, approached Mort with the idea of making a small independent film about his life. Within the first few minutes of this meeting Mort had taken what was a low-budget independent project and transformed it into a multimillion-dollar Hollywood blockbuster. We left his studio saying that at least we tried.

Mort walks into the restaurant at exactly the appointed hour dressed in his trademark blue seersucker suit and bow tie. I note that he isn't carrying a camera, but that assumption later proves to be wrong.

I begin by asking Mort his age. I immediately realize I've started off on the wrong foot when he quickly responds, "I'd rather not get into the age thing. The minute someone knows your age they put you in a category and forget about you. I've always avoided talking about my age my whole adult life."

Then he tells that his mother, May, will turn 106 this February. "I visit her several times a week, and the first thing she'll tell me is to shave off my beard or to get a better-looking suit. I guess I'll always be her little boy." He then adds, "Nobody has ever said to me, 'Mort, let's go back into your past and talk about you' . . . nobody has done that before."

I'm starting to feel like Ralph Edwards, host of 'This is Your Life.'

Mort and his younger sister grew up in New York City, where his mother worked as a fur model. "There wasn't much money, but there was always food on the table. My father died when I was eight. I don't really remember him, but I recently found an old photo of him wearing a straw hat, and I want to restore it." He often remarks that he wishes he had a father in his life. "I always hoped that my mother would remarry and I'd have a stepfather, someone to offer me guidance and reassurance, but it never happened."

Mort orders the Asian Pear and Beet Salad and explains, "I've been a vegetarian for forty years. I don't drink alcohol, no caffeine, and I swim each morning for thirty minutes. I go to the Mayo Clinic every two years for a complete physical." (I'm thinking I should ask him to drop and do fifty pushups, but how can I ask someone his age - whatever it is - to do something I can't do myself?)

Mort's story begins in the 1930s when he was a salesman for a Manhattan photographer; and at this point he stops talking to say, "Now you're going to start doing the math." I promise him I won't.

Because of his success as a salesman, he spent little time in the studio learning the nuts and bolts of photography. As this was his primary objective, he soon left to join forces with another photographer. He began taking photos at nightclubs, such as The Stork Club and Copacabana, and eventually arranged to have more than two dozen clubs on retainer at twenty-five dollars per week.

This led to getting the banquet concession at the Waldorf Astoria, where he presold his photos for $2 apiece, with a money-back guarantee if the client didn't like it. "My partner and I would come back to the office and dump all the money in a barrel," he recalls.

In 1942, Mort went into the Army, where he served in the motion-picture unit traveling around the country making training films. When he was discharged four years later, he was dismayed to discover that rent in Manhattan had tripled.

Instead of re-establishing himself in the city, he took a job at the Lido Beach Hotel on Long Island, which offered him ten weeks of work during the summer, taking photographs of guests and their families. "I had a small office, a darkroom in the basement and a bedroom on the roof where, when it rained, my bed got wet." Realizing that summer in New York was short-lived, Mort followed his clientele to Palm Beach during the winter of 1947 and moved to the island permanently in 1961. As I had once spotted Mort driving a beautiful old Rolls Royce Silver Cloud, I ask about his indulgences.

"Some people hang art on their walls, I park mine in an air-conditioned garage," he answers. "I love cars. My first car was a Model T that I bought for seven dollars, and now I own a 1921 Model T. One day I was driving that car down North Lake Way and I saw Henry Ford II. I stopped to show him the car, and then he asked me for a ride saying that he couldn't remember ever riding in one. There I was, giving a Ford a ride in a Ford. . . . I wish I had a picture of that! I also have over 100 bow ties."

Mort was briefly married in 1974, and his son Coby is a recent graduate of Rollins College. "Before I closed my studio on Peruvian Avenue I had hoped my son would come into the business," he says. "It just didn't work out."

He abruptly stops speaking. I leave well enough alone and inquire about his "brunch club." "Getting together with six or eight of my closest friends for Sunday brunch is my way of entertaining," he explains.

One of Mort's brunch buddies, Norman LeBeau, a former jeweler who is now a full-time sculptor calls Mort Kaye "the best friend anybody could have." He says Mort is misunderstood. "People think Mort is only about the buck, but it's not about the money, it's a way to keep busy," LeBeau says. "Without photography, he'd die." LeBeau ends the conversation by quoting the adage: "You can't choose your family, but you can choose your friends. And one more thing - Mort's a mensch."

Mort repeatedly tells me that he'll never stop working, he'll never retire. He attributes his longevity to his love of photography, diet, exercise and genetics. "When I closed the studio [in 2001], I expected to do four or five jobs a week. Now I'm doing four to five jobs a day!"

Mort also tells me that his mother worked as a bookkeeper for his business until she turned 99. "I would pick her up every morning at 7:15 to bring her to work." (Now I'm thinking I should submit Mort and his mother to the Guinness Book of World Records - but I'm not sure in what category.)

As we split dessert, Mort notices another photographer in the dining room. She is standing on two chairs with a camera pointed at a bowl of soup set on the table below. Mort tells me he doesn't recognize her and when she steps down, he summons her over to our table. I make the introductions as the identification badge she is wearing tells me her name is Uma Sanghvi and she works for the Palm Beach Post. Mort inquires about her schooling and former employment. He then asks her if she realizes how lucky she is to be working here. "This is the best place in the world. This is paradise!" Uma obviously is very entertained by this impromptu interrogation but excuses herself to get back to the bowl of soup. Mort then tells me how exciting it is to see someone so young who is enthusiastic and excited about her work - "just like me!"

It has been two hours since we sat down, and we both have afternoon commitments. As I begin to stand, Mort tells me to sit back down and look to my left. Out of his jacket pocket comes a compact Olympus Stylus point-and-shoot camera. "Michael, this could be the best photo taken of you in your lifetime."

RESERVATIONS

Long before Hotels.com, Expedia or Orbitz, my father had his own technique for travel - he'd just show up. No reservations, no confirmation numbers, no itinerary. I have numerous childhood memories of standing alongside him at the front desk of the Fontainebleau Hotel in Miami, the El San Juan in Puerto Rico or the St. Regis in New York City and listening to the following conversation:

Hotel clerk: "Yes, may I help you?"

My father: "Reservation for Price."

Hotel clerk: "I'm sorry sir, I don't see a reservation under that name."

My father: "Well, there must be a mistake, we'll need a room for a week."

Hotel clerk: "I'm sorry, we're fully booked."

My father: "I'd like to see the manager."

The manager would then dutifully walk out and see an imposing 6-foot-4-inch farmer from upstate New York and his dorky adolescent son standing next to him.

Manager: "May I be of assistance?"

My father: "Are you telling me that if the president of the United States walked into this hotel tonight you would not have a room for him?"

Manager: "I'm sure we could find a room for the president, sir."

My father: "I've got news for you. The president won't be staying here tonight and I'll take his room."

To add insult to injury, that was usually just the beginning. Once we were shown our accommodations, my father would find something about it he didn't like: the wallpaper, the paintings or the shower nozzle not having enough jets. He would ask to be shown another room. Once I got over the embarrassment, I accepted this as a normal operating procedure for a mildly dysfunctional family.

Eight years ago I went on a vacation to the Azores and could find only two pages in an obscure Portugal travel guide dedicated to the nine islands to help me plan my trip. A Google search today listed 706,000 hits for the Azore Islands. Whenever I find myself traveling, I'm carrying reams of printed pages containing hotel confirmation numbers, airline itineraries and rental car agreements. Even a trip to Miami necessitates a Mapquest printout.

A few weeks ago my wife and I were in Seattle visiting our son, an Army Ranger stationed at Fort Lewis. After planning a get-together with friends who live in the area, we realized it was a Saturday night and we hade little hope of getting a reservation at one of the more fashionable restaurants.

Then, I said to myself, "What would my father do?"

I won't go into detail, but we were seated at a great table by 8 p.m. on a Saturday night at one of Seattle's hottest restaurants.

Hey, who needs the Internet when you have chutzpah?

PHONE RINGS AT 3 A.M., AND AM I GLAD TO HEAR IT

When I got a phone call and my son said, "Dad, I'm suspending my cell-phone service for a while so you won't be able to get in touch with me," it could only mean one thing - deployment, U.S. Army style. The only other information he was allowed to offer was, "It will be cold."

It was futile to ask where exactly he was going, when he'll be back or if he'll be able to contact us once he gets to wherever he is going. "Any chance you can e-mail us?" I asked. "Sure, most caves have Internet access," he answered. Before he hung up, I heard him shout, "Don't forget the magazines on the balcony!" I said, "Hey, great idea, Des. Bring some reading materials for the plane.""Not those kind of magazines, moron," he responded.

That old TV ad, "It's 10 p.m., do you know where your kids are?" starts to take on a whole new meaning. I sleep most nights with the cordless phone next to the bed just in case, and sure enough at 3 a.m. last week the phone rings. "Hey, it's me. I'm in _____." (We are told his exact location is classified information.) I'm trying to awaken from a deep slumber and I try to think who I know in _____. My second thought is, "What a clear connection!"

My son tells me he has been on a cycle of 10-day missions in the mountains and currently is resting at an airfield base. "It's awesome!" he says. "We've been buying all kinds of souvenirs from the villagers. I got Mom some beautiful fabric and I bought an antique sword. I've taken over 200 photos with my digital camera, too." "Had a chance to get in any skiing?" I ask. He can't tell me anything more specific. Yes, his platoon has been fired on. "We take care of that," he says. Also, "There is a chance I'll be home for Christmas." His allotted five minutes are soon up. I tell him to be careful and not to do anything stupid. "Don't worry," he answers.

The other day I went out and bought my first flagpole. The next time I give directions to my house, instead of saying, "Look for the yellow fire hydrant at the end of the driveway," I'll say, "Look for the flagpole with both the American and the Army Ranger Regiment flags flying from it."

That sounds a whole lot better.

A DECIDEDLY PREMATURE OBITUARY

If you're anything like me, you start your morning by reading the obituaries. This works out just fine in our house because my wife likes to grab the comics first.

Before I actually read any of the departeds' biographies, I scan the page for unusual nicknames. I can usually bet on at least one Tiny, who judging from his photo may not have been so tiny. Slim, Bubbles, Smiley, Sweet Pea, Junior, Rocky and Dusty all seem fairly prevalent among the deceased. My all time favorite is "Cementhead." Now that must have been one hard-headed fellow.

Personally, I like the bios that are short and sweet. Born, died and don't bother with the flowers. In fact, my mother who recently turned 75 and hasn't been sick a day in her life, just informed me that she has made arrangements with the University of Miami to donate her remains to the medical school when she passes on.

"No service, no burial, no nothing. The only cost you'll have to pay is the transportation of my body to Miami," she told me. Then I asked her if I could save a few bucks if I drove her body down there myself. "Don't be ridiculous!" she exclaimed, "OK," I quipped, "how about Tri-Rail?"

Then my real pet peeve: the photo. The deceased died at age 99, but the photo was taken when they graduated from high school. I'm all for vanity, but when you're dead, what's the use? To spare my loved ones the last-minute creative torment of writing my obituary, I'm doing it now.

And, by the way, I'm requesting the photo be one from my high school graduation.

MICHAEL I. PRICE

Born on Mother's Day, 1956, in Hudson, N.Y., a city historically known for whaling and prostitution. At age five, he unscrewed all of the kitchen cabinet doors from their hinges, indicating a predisposition for the use of power tools.

Attended John L. Edwards Elementary School, where in third grade he was voted Class Clown. In fourth grade, he survived an acute appendicitis attack in spite of the fact his teacher thought his writhing on the floor all day was just a ploy to gain attention and make his classmates laugh.

At age 13, he received the Red Cross Junior Life Saving Certificate, despite being reprimanded for incorrect hand positioning on a female instructor during a training drill. Passed his New York state driver license test on his 16th birthday. Crashed his father's new Ford Thunderbird one day after receiving his driver license. In 1972, he attended his first Allman Brothers concert at the Saratoga Performing Arts Center, forgot where he had parked his father's car, thus began his lifelong fascination with bicycles.

Barely graduated from high school in 1974 and then began his meteoric rise up the corporate ladder. Started working as a furniture refinisher at Claire's Restoration Barn in Mellenville, N.Y. Promotions led to work as fruit picker at Mountain Range Farm, jewelry polisher at Twin Fish Jewelers, cabdriver for Star City Cab Co., graphic designer at The Wappingers Falls Press and as photographer's assistant at the Herb Sculnick Studio in New York City.

After leaving the Sculnick Studio started his own company, Michael I. Price Photography, and soon had his first photo in a national publication: His eight-months pregnant wife in overalls for Mothering magazine. Despite ongoing rejections from other major publications, such as Pigeon Journal and Scrap Metal Monthly, his perseverance led to assignments from People, Newsweek, The New York Times and USA Today.

In 1986, he was hired by the Palm Beach Daily News as a staff photographer, irrespective of the fact that chief photographer Kim Sargent told then-publisher Agnes Ash that "I never in my life saw someone wearing clothes so wrinkled." Within days of starting his new job, he purchased a pair of Nike Air Jordan red leather sneakers, which were to become his trademark.

After working two seasons and consuming approximately eight-hundred cheese puff pastries, four-hundred crab claws, eighty pounds of shrimp, and countless carrot and celery sticks, he resigned to work as a full-time freelance photographer. His career immediately soared when thespian and local resident Burt Reynolds threatened to "rip his head off" for taking his photo while on the set of B.L. Stryker, one of many Reynolds' cancelled TV endeavors.

Riding the momentum of the Reynolds' shoot, he then went on to photograph such luminaries as Donna Mills, star of the TV drama series Knot's Landing; Vice President Dan Quayle; and Beverly Hills hair stylist with the cowboy hat and ponytail, Jose Eber.

Although Mr. Price never formally retired, he spent his remaining years watching reruns of Law & Order and fabricating crucifixes from discarded engine parts. He was often heard saying, "When the running was good, I ran hard," which his friends believe was a reference to the 1970s and early 1980s.

READY TO WEAR

I'm not sure when my aversion to wearing a dress shirt, necktie and sport jacket began, but it may have been when I was eight years old. My father, who was raised on a farm in upstate New York and later worked as an accountant and realtor in a small agricultural community, dressed for work each day in a dry-cleaned, freshly starched white shirt, silk necktie and custom-tailored blazer. None of this would have seemed unusual other than the fact that most of his contemporaries wore denim overalls and flannel shirts.

My memory of being coerced to put on that stiff-collared polyester shirt and clip-on tie is right up there with my first filling at the dentist, my first booster shot at the pediatrician and putting my finger into the glowing red-hot car cigarette lighter at my cousin Bobby Saperstein's suggestion. To my family's dismay, my loathing of corporate clothing would prevent me from pursuing a career as a lawyer, banker, Secret Service agent, politician or television news anchor.

When I came to Palm Beach to work at the Shiny Sheet, one of my first requirements was to purchase a tuxedo, something I didn't recall was in the job description. In addition, I didn't realize that most tuxes are made of wool! I made it through the first season, but I was able to gradually customize my uniform with black linen pants, a thrift-store Armani jacket and a Banana Republic black cotton shirt.

Eventually, it occurred to me that, as long as I was taking someone's photo and they could expect it to appear in print, they didn't care if I was wearing a green terrycloth thong, fishnet tank top and cowboy boots.

Which brings me to my point. It is very unlikely that you will be judged by your clothes in Palm Beach. Bruce Strickland, maitre'd at Cafe L'Europe, admits he would have a hard time allowing someone with cut-off shorts and a T-shirt to gain entry (he did turn away Sweatin' With the Oldies advocate Richard Simmons for appearing exactly like that), but confessed there are always exceptions to the rule. "If it was Brad Pitt I wouldn't have a problem." Strickland added, "It's the jewelry, not the clothes."

Ten years ago, Renato's kept a supply of jackets in case a gentleman showed up without one, but today maitre'd Brad Stapleton expects his younger and more fashionable clientele to dress more casually. "Especially with our outdoor dining, it doesn't make a lot of sense to be dressed so formally. The restaurant was full of rocket scientists last night, and not one was wearing a tie," explained Stapleton, who I noted was wearing a green wool blazer with an Hermes tie.

If you happen to spot art dealer John Surovek at a black-tie event, at first glance it may appear that he forgot to put on his pants, but he is probably wearing his custom-made tuxedo shorts. "Since Palm Beach is a town known for haute couture and being somewhat creative, I thought it was time to lead the way with sartorial splendor," he said. Surovek admits that "most people were initially perplexed, but now when I wear long pants people assume I've been to a funeral."

Speaking of funerals, I mention the late Neil Cargile and Surovek takes a long pause and responds, "Now there's a guy whose high heels are tough to fill." Neil, a Palm Beach mining executive who died in 1995, etched a lasting impression in my mind and I'm sure in countless others. I met him at one of the island's pubs in the 1980s when he asked my wife for a dance. The top half of him looked typical Palm Beach: Brooks Brothers navy blue blazer, white oxford button-down shirt, necktie. It wasn't until I glanced down that I noticed he was wearing a black Ann Taylor miniskirt, fishnet stockings and dark pumps. He may have also been carrying a small Judith Leiber handbag.

Later I overheard Neil explaining to someone who obviously was having a difficult time understanding his attire: "If you aren't doing something different, you aren't doing anything at all." I admired Neil even though I thought his sense of color at times seemed garish and his makeup a bit heavy-handed. At his funeral, a local hairstylist fondly remembered him by stating, "He was the type of theme dresser who could cross-dress in society here and be accepted by everyone." Amen.

I was recently refused admittance to a restaurant/nightclub in the northern end of Palm Beach County because I was wearing a shirt without a collar (never mind I was also wearing a sport coat) and red leather Bally sneakers. Normally, I would never have presented myself at such an establishment, but I was invited by a saxophonist who was playing there with a group of local musicians. (He lives in the area, but tours with a singer named Bruce from New Jersey). I asked for the manager and explained my situation. At the end, he said, "I'll let it go this time, but not again." "Don't worry," I said. "I won't be back."

As the saying goes, "It's the clothes that make the man," but Palm Beachers have the sense to know that it's really the man that makes the clothes.

SUMMER VACATIONS

When I was a kid growing up in Hudson, New York, a small, depressed town along the banks of the Hudson River, I dreaded summer vacation. I would watch my neighbors and friends pack up their station wagons and escape to the cool waters of Cape Cod, the crisp mountain air of the Adirondacks or the tranquility of Lake Champlain. As for my family, each August we trekked due south, to one of the hottest cities in America: Miami Beach.

I would ask my father why we couldn't go to Florida during Christmas vacation instead, and I would get the often-repeated lecture, "When I was a kid, " he would begin, "I never got a summer vacation. I worked on my parents' farm picking fruit for 2 cents a bushel." My Aunt Millie informed me that my father liked to exaggerate about his toils on the farm - he was actually paid 3 cents a bushel.

In any case, when my father turned 18 he immediately enlisted in the Navy. I assume he was fed up with all that fruit picking. Eventually, it was explained that the only time my father, who was then an accountant, could leave work was in the middle of summer. As for why we went to Miami, I can only assume it had something to do with the reduced off-season room rates.

One summer, I remember walking down Collins Avenue thinking, "Gee, it really is hot enough to fry an egg on the sidewalk." Which isn't to say it was all that bad. One day Cassius Clay, who was training at a gym in Miami Beach, stopped in the hotel lobby and signed autographs. My father took a picture of us together, but that one, along with most of the photos of my younger brother, have been misplaced.

I also remember Gary Puckett and the Union Gap sitting around the hotel pool after a concert. Then there were the summer riots. It seemed that there was always something going on in Miami, even back then.

Eventually, we stopped going to Florida for our summer vacation. My parents decided that four weeks at Camp Pontiac in the Berkshires, Mass., would not only benefit me, but would give them a few weeks of peace and quiet as well.

When visiting on Parent's Day, they learned that I was the first camper to earn both the Dolphin Swimmer Certificate and the NRA Junior Marksmanship Medal in one summer. When I came home and insisted that they buy me my own Winchester rifle, they determined that I had enough of the summer camp experience.

The summers my family stayed home were just fine with me. I tinkered with lawn mower engines trying to make something with two wheels that I wouldn't have to pedal. I took a 4-H tractor safety course. I even was invited to join friends on their family vacations.

One summer I went to Martha's Vineyard with Sandi, who was a nanny for a family from New York City. Although I was only 16, I had a fake ID, and one night I suggested we go out to the bars after the kids were put to bed. The next morning Sandi wasn't feeling all that well, and for some reason I wasn't invited back the following summer.

I can't say for sure, but my required attendance at summer school may have put a lid on any further family vacation plans. I was also instructed to find a job for the summer, something along the lines of picking fruit for 2 cents a bushel.

After torturously sitting through three hours of remedial Spanish, I would jump on my bicycle and pedal three miles to Hudson Valley Ford. Once there, I would grab a sponge and bucket, and wash cars for the next four hours. One afternoon, Herb, the senior car-detailing technician, came up to me and said, "Mike, I've been watching you and you've been doing a great job. I've decided to let you wash Mr. M's car every afternoon. When you vacuum the interior, under no circumstance should you reach under the driver's seat."

Mr. M was the owner of the dealership and also owned a vending machine company. That, and the fact his last named ended in a vowel, linked him to membership in a certain "family," at least in my mind. Of course the first thing I did once I started to vacuum the interior was reach under the front seat. I felt a smooth, metal, pistol-shaped object which was in fact a .45 caliber Smith & Wesson snub-nosed revolver.

I always made sure there weren't any water spots on the hood of that particular black Lincoln Continental.

When it came time for my wife and me to plan our summer vacations, I tried not to repeat the mistakes my parents made. The phrase "family vacation" was an oxymoron in our house. For the sake of our son, we tried to make our summer vacations a "cultural experience."

When Desmond was 7, he spent two summer weeks in rural India watching MTV at a new friend's house while his mother was back at the ashram on her knees praying for a bottle of Immodium. When he was 10, he got lost in the Rastro, the largest flea market in Madrid. We waited on a street corner for what seemed hours as tens of thousands shuffled past. The expression "kidnapped by gypsies" wasn't far from our minds. Finally we spotted a bright red sweatshirt and watched in disbelief as he calmly walked past us, oblivious of our panic and his possible danger.

There were other escapades in Ecuador, Mexico, Russia and Eastern Europe; he has a clear memory of none of them. In fact, because we dragged him around so much, he now hates to travel.

For our summer vacation this year, my wife and I are planning to do something we have always talked about but have never done. We're unplugging the clocks, disconnecting the phones, and stashing away the car keys. We'll ride our bikes to Publix, read books, rent movies, swim and take naps. We always say we live in paradise, and this summer we're going to Shangri-La, otherwise known as our back yard.

PIPE DREAMS

I tried everything. First the plunger, then the auger, then the snake and finally the drain cleaner with the forbidding skull and crossbones on the label. In a final moment of desperation I even called my friend Robert, a true connoisseur of the commode, and held the phone receiver in the bowl hoping he could audibly diagnose my problem. No such luck. It was time to call in the big guns.

Two hours after I called Rapid Rooter, a young man who introduced himself as Jason was standing on my doorstep. I would have shaken his outstretched hand, but after noticing he was wearing latex gloves, I opted to verbally welcome him into my home.

After a few minutes of running tests, Jason informed me he had gotten to the bottom of my problem. Beginning with the proverbial 'good news/bad news,' I learned that it wasn't Ficus roots that had invaded the sewer pipe, just toilets that had seen their better days.

"Your toilets are 40 years old, and have so much mineral buildup that they can't function properly. It would be cheaper for you to go out and buy two new toilets than to try to repair these old ones," Jason informed me. I couldn't resist replying, "You mean it would be like flushing money down the toilet to try to fix them?" Jason's expression told me this wasn't the first time he had heard that response.

While Jason was packing up his tools I tried to mentally prepare myself for what was to come next. With checkbook in hand, I asked, "What do I owe you for the service call?" Nothing on this Earth could have prepared me for his answer: "Nothing." I was bowled over. Jason left me his business card and told me if I needed someone to install my new toilets to give him a call.

Two weeks later my two new specially ordered Kohler Wellworths arrived at Home Depot and I gleefully contacted Jason to schedule the installation. Coincidentally, the day we selected was also our 24th wedding anniversary.

If you happened to have been driving down Marlin Road on July 19, you may have noticed two toilets, one baby blue, the other Pepto pink, sitting at the end of our driveway, waiting for the garbage truck to carry them off to the great "cuarto de bano" in the sky. I can't say we had tears in our eyes, but it was sad to see our two companions leave us after sharing so much time together. A few minutes later, like a perfectly orchestrated ballet, a crane and dump truck arrived to haul our two friends away. Flushed with emotion, I turned to my wife and said, "Happy anniversary, darling."

I'VE GOT YOUR NUMBER

When I met Jim Hansen, owner of Hansen Landscaping, sixteen years ago, he told me his phone number and said, "Mike, you'll never forget it, I promise you."

I may have called him only once or twice in all these years, but he was right. His phone number: 832-TREE. My massage therapist, Karen, also has a phone number that is almost impossible for me to forget: 844-9111. (Yes, Karen, this is an emergency! My lower back is really sore!)

I've always been envious of people who have easy-to-remember numbers, ones in which all four digits in the suffix are the same. My friend, Joan, told me that because she knew someone who worked at BellSouth, she was able to get one of those numbers anyone can recall. Of course, I had no such luck. I can't even recollect my own phone number, let alone expect someone else to.

Even though rotary phones were once staples in my life, my grandmother had an additional hardship: a party line. It seemed whenever I needed to make a call, I'd pick up the phone and Mr. Lambert, the farmer down the road, was gabbing away about the high cost of chicken feed or the problems with his manure spreader.

I would ask my grandmother why she just couldn't get her own private line like everyone else, but that would bring on a sermon about the Great Depression, the value of a penny saved, a penny earned or what life was like before electricity or phones.

I can remember my first home phone number, 828-1107. The best part about that number was that one of our local pizza parlors, The Pizza Pit, had a similar number. When I was old enough to baby-sit for my younger brother, I couldn't wait for my parents to go out on Saturday nights. I would invite my friend, Jim, over and wait for the phone to ring.

"Hello, Pizza Pit, can I take your order? Tomato sauce is an extra charge tonight. You want cheese on that pizza, too?" Sometimes we would take the order as requested and then call the competing pizza emporium, The Paramount Grill. We would then order a pizza using the unsuspecting caller's address.

The catch was, the Paramount Grill served a square pizza that was baked on a piece of cardboard, and it tasted like it, too. Jim and I would imagine the confusion when the pizza was delivered: "I thought I ordered from the Pizza Pit?"

Before the days of Caller ID and Star 69, I would often partake in what was once known as the prank phone call: "Is your refrigerator running? You'd better go catch it." Or dialing up the local tobacconist, "Do you have Prince Albert in a can? Then you'd better let him out!" All fairly harmless, unless these exploits happened to take place between the hours of midnight and 2 a.m.

I lived in a village in upstate New York that had the distinction of being one of only a handful of municipalities in the country with a privately owned phone company. What this meant was anytime I made a call outside a five-mile radius of my home, an operator would come on the line and ask me for my phone number. This was for billing purposes. The operator was usually Cathy, a girl I sat next to in 10th-grade algebra. Fortunately, all those calls to California never did show up on my monthly phone bill.

My friend, Judy, recently related a story about a potential windfall pertaining to her phone number. In late 1970s, she was a student at Morris County Community College in New Jersey and worked the midnight shift at a Dunkin' Donuts.

One bleary-eyed morning she received a call from MacNeil Laboratories asking if she would sell them her phone number. Apparently her number spelled TYLENOL. Barely awake, she asked what dollar figure they were willing to offer, and then settled on a figure not much more than several hundred dozen glazed doughnuts. Today, her phone number is one digit different from that of a local television station, and she often receives tips on "breaking news" or "Crimestoppers," which she happily forwards.

On a lark, I decided to call 655-1111, a number I consider very desirable. Dr. David Haughton, an optometrist in Palm Beach, answered the phone. Although he was on his way to a Kiwanis meeting, he was more than willing to give me the 411.

He told me he obtained his number in 1964, when it was changed from another number that had been issued to his father in 1928. "I wanted to keep the original number, and a honcho with the phone company was a patient of mine," Haughton said. "He told me there was no way to keep my old number. I was given a choice of any number up to 2000, and decided the easiest number to dial on a rotary phone was 1111."

I asked Haughton if he had even been approached to sell his number. "I'd sell it for half a million dollars and then retire," he told me. Before he hung up, I forgot to ask him if he has call waiting.

A LESSON LEARNED

There was a day, not so long ago, that I too was as guilty as Martha Stewart. I was 14 years old, a student at Hudson Junior High. Spring was in the air, summer vacation was just around the corner, and what better time, I decided, to skip a day of school. I recruited Billy Clarke, who had the unsettling distinction of having both long hair and being "quiet," and Joe Concra, whose parents ran the Paramount Grill.

My family would often patronize Joe's family's establishment, where the pizza was square and tasted mildly of the cardboard it was served on. In any case, I suggested to Joe that he grab a six-pack of Pabst Blue Ribbon to help us celebrate our furlough. I would bring the bologna sandwiches.

The plan was simple: We would meet at the ball field behind the school just before the first homeroom bell, then sneak off into the woods and walk down to the railroad tracks along the river. Around 2:30, just before recess, we would return to the campus and then walk home as though we had been in school all day. I later remembered thinking that I would have been less bored if I had actually attended classes.

My father would arrive home from work at 5 p.m., and I vividly recall standing in the driveway when he pulled up, got out of his car, and asked me, "How was school today?" I didn't detect anything unusual, so I answered him, "Just fine." When we sat down to dinner later that evening he started in: "How was math class? How was English? How was social studies? How was gym class?"

I looked up from my plate and noted the veins in his forehead started to pulsate. I knew my world was starting to slowly unravel and I'd have to think quickly. "Well, actually, Dad I wasn't feeling so good, so I spent most of the day in the nurse's office." "Were Billy and Joe sick too?" he shouted.

If I had had a lawyer standing next to me, I would have taken the Fifth. In what only could be described as a display of my father's Hungarian temper, his hand came crashing down on the table. All the plates and food shot up in the air, just like in the cartoons. For my mother and younger brother, it must have been like watching someone walking to the gallows and hanging himself. Look out, Dead Student Walking.... My father was soon on the phone talking to Billy's mother. What I hadn't accounted for was that Billy's aunt was also the school nurse. Let's just say the next few weeks weren't the happiest.

Did I learn my lesson? I'd like to think so. Whenever I got caught doing something wrong, if I readily admitted it, I often found that the punishment was much less severe than if I had tried to lie my way out of it. My Aunt Millie often told me stories about my father, punctuating the last sentence with, "He was no angel either, but he always told the truth."

This got me thinking about my own son. In kindergarten, he locked his teacher in the closet while fifteen 6-year-olds howled hysterically. The teacher was finally rescued by the principal, who suggested my son might be better suited for another school. The following year at Palm Beach Public School, he was asked by his first-grade teacher to draw a portrait of her, which he did, rendering her in the nude. But for all his misdeeds, he readily took full responsibility. For that, I had to commend him, although not without some minor punishment.

As for Martha, if only she had learned one of life's most valuable lessons sooner. Maybe if she had skipped school more often.

BIKE LANE: NO-BRAINER

I can't imagine who, in their right mind, would be against adding a few feet of asphalt to widen State Road A1A. Unless, of course, you happen to be one of the few property owners who have encroached on the state-owned right-of-way and can't bear giving up a newly planted ficus hedge.

Bob Eigelberger, an avid bicyclist who also is known to be outspoken on any number of issues, recently expressed his opinion: "The bike lane is not an option, it is the law in the state of Florida and it's about time that those living along A1A realize that it is a state highway and there are laws that prevail." Now if only a little common sense would prevail as well.

For those who haven't had the experience of riding a bicycle along one of South Florida's most scenic thoroughfares, let me summarize it in one word: terrifying.

Scenario No. 1: You're riding along A1A, hugging the white line because there is no shoulder. A Ford Excursion SUV with the optional extra large break-away side mirrors comes bearing down on you. Behind the wheel is a soccer mom hyped up on her third cup of double-latte-iced-frappeed cappuccino of the day. The kids behind her in the fifth-row seating are screaming because they can't find the Barney DVD, her Palm Pilot is beeping to remind her she is late for her radioactive-mud foot wrap, the cell phone remote earpiece is caught on her Cartier watchband, and to make matters worse, the Pilates workout earlier in the day was much too strenuous.

As the mirror hits you in the head, it folds back against the passenger window so she can't look back and see you on the ground.

Scenario No. 2: You're riding your bicycle along A1A, hugging the white line because there is no shoulder. A Mercury Marquis with a blue handicapped parking tag dangling from the rear-view mirror comes bearing down on you. Behind the wheel is a man wearing large, dark wrap-around sunglasses because he had cataract surgery two days ago. In the passenger seat is his wife of seventy-five years. The wife screams, "Watch out for the guy on the bicycle!" He replies, "What bicycle?"

Scenario No. 3: You're riding your bicycle along A1A, hugging the white line because there is no shoulder. A pickup covered in concrete dust, rust and NRA bumper stickers comes bearing down on you.

Behind the wheel is a guy who just spent eight hours tarring a roof, he broke up with his girlfriend the night before (she has custody of the pit bull), his bowling team is in last place, and to add insult to injury, the engine on the bass boat needs a new head gasket. I can hear him saying to himself, "Maybe I'll feel a whole lot better if I throw this beer can at that fellow riding a bicycle." I'm thankful he wasn't drinking magnums of Dom Perignon.

Although these are obvious exaggerations, everyone has had distractions while driving. The recipes for disaster are endless. Of course, I also agree that the $50 million price tag for a bike lane seems a bit steep, but it's hard to put a price on someone's life. And you needn't look any further than the airport flyover at Interstate 95 to see how easy it is to waste $250 million of taxpayer money on a project that wasn't needed and for which the taxpayers hadn't asked.

Mike Zingaro, a professional cyclist who trains each morning on A1A, has plenty of harrowing tales. Near-misses, run off the road, milkshakes thrown at him. "I can't understand why this is even an issue," he says. "What I'm worried about is the people who ride for recreation once or twice a week and they're stuck out there with the traffic. It makes sense for the cyclist and for the motorist alike to have a bike lane. How could anyone not want one?"

My guess is he hasn't spoken to any of the property owners along A1A yet. Manalapan Town Commissioner Peter Blum told The Palm Beach Post earlier this year that, "I think it [A1A] should be a scenic highway and shouldn't be widened at all. All it does is make people want to speed a little bit more. Bicyclists have all the rights everyone else has. Maybe they ought to have licenses like cars." Now there's a politician who knows his constituents.

Peter Burt, a Palm Beach resident who spends most weekends competing in triathlons, says he believes statements such as those made by Commissioner Blum reflect an ignorance of the situation. "What people don't understand is that it's a safety issue, and the bicyclists deserve the extra road. If anyone thinks otherwise, it's for their own selfish gain," Burt says.

The debate will no doubt go on for sometime. Rest assured there will be many more injuries and possibly deaths. It remains to be seen if a bike lane will be built along A1A. If Henry Flagler had ever said, "Go south, young man," he surely didn't mean by bicycle along State Road A1A.

HOUSE GUESTS

Sooner or later we all get them. The incubation period begins in December, and by January many of us are experiencing the full-blown symptoms of Housitosum guestsus northesis, more commonly known as "house guests from up North."

The first sign of trouble is a phone call. "Hey Mike, this is Shawn from Montpelier. It's 15 below zero, and that's without the wind chill. What's the temperature in Palm Beach?" I now have two choices. Either I can pretend my phone just died and terminate the connection, or face the inevitable and say, "Eighty degrees and not a cloud in the sky. When exactly are you thinking about coming down?"

Along with perennial house guests come their quirky habits. My buddy Shawn has always been preoccupied with his personal hygiene. However, his three showers a day along with a load or two of laundry is too much for my hot water heater and my wallet. I also can count on my electric bill to double, which makes me think it may be cheaper to put him up in a hotel.

A week after his last departure Shawn sent me a large package containing a case of Scottish Country Soap, each bar wrapped in fine tissue paper. Either he was feeling a bit guilty or just planning ahead for his next visit. Just in case, I contacted FPL and scheduled a free energy audit.

Another friend from high school, Dave, the Kirsch curtain rod heir, seems to have a motivation problem. One day his own mother told him, "Dave, you're a thinker, not a doer." She wasn't kidding. In the countless times he has stayed with us, I have never seen him "do" a dirty dish or make his bed. His wit, humor and unlimited useless knowledge of trivia make up for those shortcomings. But more often than not, as I trip over his wet towel, his impending departure fills me with a sense of dread . . . about discovering what he's left behind.

You also can count on the obligatory winter visit from a family member. My brother-in-law, Dick, who lives in Spirit Lake, Idaho, recently made a pilgrimage to South Florida. I called him before he left home and advised, "Lose the red-and-black checkered flannel shirt and brown corduroy pants. Pack shorts, and don't forget a nice pair of khakis, collared shirt and blazer in case we decide to skip Taco Bell one night and go to Echo for sushi."

It wasn't until we were sitting at our table waiting for the blue fin tuna sampler that Dick said, "I never had sushi before." Normally I wouldn't have found such an admittance so startling, but this is a guy who spent six months on a Japanese fishing trawler cruising around in the Bering Sea monitoring fish quotas for the U.S. government. If Dick comes back next year, I promised him we'd go to Cafe L'Europe for some fish eggs on toast. The remainder of his visit was spent indoors or swaddled head to toe in sun-proof garments, because of his sensitivity to the ultraviolet rays.

There is nothing like a house guest from Switzerland who constantly reminds you that life is so much better back in Europe. My friends Bernard and Marianne from Geneva have thoughtfully corrected us on: how to properly set a table for dinner; how to fold the dish towels; what cheese we should eat and what toothpaste we need to use.

Granted, they always arrive with a supply of chocolates and Swiss Army penknives as presents, and expecting a Patek Phillipe is asking too much. At least they limit themselves to five-minute showers.

My friend Butch, who has a house in Palm Beach with seven bathrooms, once told me, "When it comes to house guests, you can never have enough facilities." Robert, one of my high school sidekicks, would agree. Back in the 1960s, he had a phobia of public restrooms and would walk two miles home from school each day at noon to use his own "private washroom." The problem was, he never walked back. Needless to say, his high school diploma was a long time in coming.

Today, in preparation for Robert's yearly visit, we dutifully clean out the "extra" bathroom tucked in the corner of our garage. Out come all the boxes, extra lawn chairs and chipped picture frames and in go a package of Charmin bathroom tissue (with aloe) and a stack of bicycling magazines. Little did we know when we purchased our home that the utility room in the garage would be such a crucial amenity.

For all the oddballs, there is one who is on the ball. Kim, my friend Craig's wife, can't stop cleaning our house each time she visits. She usually starts her morning on vacation by talking on the phone (business), making breakfast and loading the dishwasher. Eventually she moves on to sweeping the floors and washing the windows, but only after thoroughly cleaning the bathrooms, and even sometimes, the garage. By the third day she's asking us what rug shampoo we prefer for the carpet in our cars. By the time her suitcase is packed and she is on her way back to the airport, we're tearfully waving goodbye.

GRADUATION DAY

"I have never let schooling interfere with my education."
- Mark Twain (1835-1910)

This may come as a surprise, but I've yet to be asked to give a commencement address. Given the fact that I barely made it through high school and never attended an institution of higher learning, I guess I shouldn't be too disappointed.

When my younger brother, Steve, graduated from Vassar College, I stood by with my camera as Meryl Streep, an alumnus, handed him his diploma. My mother displayed that photo on her kitchen fireplace mantle for more years than I care to remember. I always wanted to know why she didn't put the picture of my father and Milton Berle next to it. That way, when I sat down to eat a corned beef sandwich, I could pretend I was at the Carnegie Deli.

Whenever someone asks me what college I graduated from, my typical answer is: The School of Hard Knocks. At one point I compiled a formidable list of friends, both successful and otherwise, who forged ahead in the world without a college diploma. That's not to say my buddy Jim, a neurosurgeon in Savannah, Ga., would have been better off getting his medical training via a correspondence course advertised in the back of Field & Stream magazine.

Another longtime acquaintance, David, amassed a fortune from real estate ventures and partnerships without taking one SAT test. There are eight U.S. presidents and ten Nobel Prize Winners who have never made it through the gates of a college campus.

I note that, about this time each year, various colleges and universities vie for the publicity generated by their commencement speaker. You can bet that neither Ted Kennedy nor Al Franken will be at the podium at West Point. Sometimes, it seems the celebrity commencement speaker is simultaneously awarded an honorary degree, a sort of added incentive. Local crooner Vic Damone dropped out of high school but returned later to earn his diploma at age sixty-eight. It appears to me that Bill Cosby keeps busy collecting honorary Ph.D.s from any educational institution willing to subject a graduating class to his redundant humor.

Self-proclaimed "Roads Scholar" and local musician Butch Trucks recently informed me that he was the keynote speaker at the Class of 2000 graduation ceremony at the Landmark School, a private secondary school on the outskirts of Boston. "That school saved my son, Seth. When I got a letter in the mail inviting me to give the commencement address, I figured if they wanted a rock 'n' roll drummer up there, no problem."

Asking him if he remembered the gist of his speech, he told me, "Basically I just winged it, but the overlying message was to follow your dreams and find your bliss." He noted that he, too, was awarded an honorary diploma, although he is already a proud graduate of Englewood High School in Jacksonville.

If one were to ask me who I would recommend as a commencement speaker for this year's graduating seniors, I'd suggest my friend Ricardo. Ricky, as he was known to his classmates, was a real anomaly in the Hudson Public School system. His mother, Bernice, was well-known in the community and in the extended reaches of Upstate New York as the proprietor of Bernice's, a local house of ill repute. In fifth grade, Ricky would normally attend class wearing a three-piece suit. That, and the fact he sported a fine-tuned mustache, gave him an air of aristocracy not normally associated with an elementary school pupil. Our teacher doled out his usual punishment on a regular basis: having us kneel with our faces pressed into the blackboard in the front of the classroom. What always made me chuckle was when Ricky would take a small piece of paper and place it on the floor as to not soil his expensive pleated trousers.

One day Ricky wasn't apparently not moving fast enough in getting to the front of the room. The teacher grabbed him by the jacket lapel, picked him up, and put him head first into the garbage can. I can only assume he was always irked by Ricky because he was a much better dresser.

Last summer while visiting a friend in my hometown, I ran into Ricky. I'm not sure I would have recognized him if not for that perfectly trimmed mustache. I learned he had fallen victim to New York's stringent drug laws back in the '70s and had been sentenced to life in prison for possessing a small amount of an illegal substance. His sentence had been recently reduced to time served, and he was back home wondering what to do with his life. Considering he just spent 25 years in a maximum security prison, he didn't look that bad. I couldn't offer him much solace, but I told him to let me know if I could help him. As we shook hands and parted, he yelled back, "Hey, at least I got my diploma!" Which isn't to say that there isn't a price to pay for 'continuing education.'

42

THE FOREMAN: HOT DOGS, CIGARETTES AND OPINIONS

On a balmy summer night last June, my friend and renowned local architect Rick Gonzalez sat in my back yard and said, "Mike, if you decide to cut down that horrendous ficus tree, I could design a small pool pavilion and pergola that would be a really nice addition to your home." Out of his shirt pocket came a pen and, on a napkin, he quickly drew a Balinese-inspired structure that was fascinating.

When I asked what a project like that would cost, his estimate seemed reasonable and realistic. Then again, it might have been the Red Stripe beers that made it appear so attractive. Today, nine months and untold dollars later, we stare out from cement dust-encrusted windows at what appears to be a gravel pit with 15-foot monolithic timbers rising from the ground.

Each weekday morning for the past month, I've been awakened at 6:30 by the semi-muffled sound of a 1979 Ford F-250 pickup pulling into my driveway. Next, my sense of smell is slowly stimulated by the aroma of fresh coffee and the waffling scent of a burning Salem.

As I lift my head off the pillow and look out into my back yard, I see him standing there; a hammer in one hand, cigarette in the other, gazing up at the dawn sky. What he's thinking about, I haven't a clue. That is, until I ask him. His name is Glenn Winkler, and he's a foreman for Kenneth Rice Construction. When we first met, his boss, Ken, introduced us by saying, "Mike, meet the newest member of your family." They both were laughing, and now I know why.

Glenn starts his work day at 4 a.m. with breakfast and the newspaper. By daybreak he's on the job site. "It's the best time of the day," he explains. "I'm the first guy there. I watch the sun come up, the beauty of Mother Nature ... total tranquility." That is, until he starts up the circular saw, compressor, jack hammer, concrete cutter, dirt compactor or any combination of the above. Just ask my neighbors.

One recent morning, I spotted Glenn leaning against his more-rust-than-green pickup eating a hot dog and drinking a magnum-size cup of Pepsi, which, at 7 a.m., seemed a bit unusual. "I got hooked on these spicy hot dogs from 7-Eleven," he said. When I question the former star athlete about his seemingly unhealthy diet and habits, he took a long drag on his cigarette and said, "My brother, who is a health teacher at

Forest Hill High School, often criticizes me, but then he's got a few extra pounds to lose himself."

If there was anybody born with a silver shovel in his mouth, it is Glenn. His father owned a successful tennis court construction and maintenance business, and Glenn spent his summer vacations sweltering away building or remodeling tennis courts in Palm Beach.

"I remember working on the tennis court at the Kennedy mansion when I was 13 or 14 years old, " he said. "My father's truck had a Nixon bumper sticker on it, and when we left that day someone had pasted a Kennedy sticker over the top of it. We never forgot that."

I always can count on a daily commentary on current events. Haiti: "There isn't a tree left in that country!" Iraq: "What the hell are we doing there?" Bush or Kerry: "Don't care. They're going to do what they're going to do." Gun control: "Every man should have a good weapon." Population growth: "It's disgusting, you can't stop it." Education: "Now the kids speak twenty-seven different languages. How can you teach somebody you can't communicate with?"

If one were to suggest his views are a little to the right of his idol John Wayne, I don't think he'd mind a bit. He's in bed by 8 p.m., which doesn't give him much time to watch The O'Reilly Factor.

Twice-divorced and an avid hunter and gardener, he has been married for the past three years to wife Deborah. She is, as he often addresses her on his midday cell phone call, "the love of my life." They met while "shooting pool," he says, and they share a passion for NASCAR, steak dinners and country-western music.

"I'm interested in relationships, and read a lot of Dr. Phil's books," he told me one day. I also learned that his wife changed her work schedule at Wackenhut Inc. so they can spend more time together. On Sundays, don't expect to find them at a polo match in Wellington - they watch NASCAR races on television. "It's incredible when you have Surround Sound," he said.

Glenn mentioned to me that he once spent five months working on a 5,000-square-foot coquina stone patio at an oceanfront mansion in Palm Beach. "I had to personally pick and lay every piece so the pattern would be consistent," he said. I thought this would be a good opportunity to pry a few additional thoughts about Palm Beach from him. Among his reflections: "People want you to work on their house, but they don't want to see you there. How else are you going to do the job?"

He also tells me that as a kid he would often hang out at the Lido

Pool or the Palm Beach Pier and even took tennis lessons at the Recreation Center. "I was part of the working class, not the rich. When I was attending Auburn University, friends would ask me, 'You're from Palm Beach?' and I'd have to say, 'No, West Palm Beach' and then explain the difference. Gucci loafers on one side, Red Wing steel-toed work boots on the other."

I often hear nightmare stories about construction projects gone awry and asked Glenn his advice for homeowners. "Quality control is almost nonexistent, and it's smart to hire someone to oversee your project," he answered. "I'd also suggest getting out the books and educating yourself."

Depending on who I listen to, my backyard pavilion project might be finished in the next week or two, or maybe it will be another month. It's anybody's guess. In either case, I'll soon have to adjust to life without Glenn. I don't want to sound overly sentimental, but I'll miss him. As for my neighbors, they're counting the days.

TRIBUTE TO MOM

Whenever I hear my mother tell the story, it always sounds like the beginning of a Charles Dickens novel.

"I was so miserable. It was one of the worst days of my life," she begins. "Back then there was no air-conditioning in hospitals. But can you imagine? What a present! I was so happy!"

The 'worst' day she is referring to is my birthday: May 13, 1956, which happened to fall on the second Sunday of May, Mother's Day. As for the spring heat wave, that was a fluke.

Things were different then. I envision my mother trading drags on a Marlboro with her obstetrician between contractions. I would often chide her about being drugged to relieve the pain. How could she even remember giving birth to me? Whenever I bring this to her attention, her usual response is, "Don't be ridiculous."

I can't recall celebrating many of my mother's first dozen or so Mother's Days; I'm sure that task fell into the hands of my father. I once made a feeble attempt to serve her breakfast in bed and later gave her a letter holder I made in shop class. But, when I would ask her what she'd like for a Mother's Day present, her traditional answer was, "Just a card and maybe not trying to drown your brother in the bathtub for once will suffice."

There was nothing worse than lying sick in bed as a child. My mother would sit beside me, at the ready with a glass of ginger ale and a stack of saltine crackers. I was especially grateful to her the day I spent writhing with stomach pain.

My father, who considered himself an unrecognized member of the medical profession, had diagnosed my problem as constipation and suggested an enema. Fortunately, my mother recommended we consult the family doctor first. I was diagnosed with acute appendicitis.

The day I turned 16, my mother took me to the courthouse so I could get my driver's permit. I didn't know it at the time, but in the space for my name, I should have written, "Slow the hell down," which I subsequently heard so often I began to think was my name. When I finally passed my driving test a short time later, my mother talked my father into letting me borrow his new Thunderbird so I could go to the dentist. Who could blame her for not knowing that another car would run a stop sign at just the exact second I was passing through?

In my later years, I would get a phone call from my father around the first week of May to remind me not to forget Mother's Day. "Remember to get your mother something nice," he would say. Since I could no longer offer to stop beating up my 6-foot, 200-pound younger brother, I could usually find a card and get it in the mail on time.

During my most recent bout with the flu, my mother drove up from Delray Beach to deliver her homemade chicken soup, a bottle of ginger ale and a box of saltine crackers. It is reassuring to know that a man on the cusp of turning 50 still needs to hear his mother tell him, "That's what you get for running around like a nut." When I most recently spoke to my son, I reminded him, like my own father did for me, that Mother's Day is approaching and he may want to plan accordingly. I took the sighs and grunts as an acknowledgment. There may be extenuating circumstances on his end, so I'll find a card and a box of Godiva chocolates just in case.

As for my mother, she prefers to wait "until all the hoopla" is over. "We'll celebrate together, your birthday and Mother's Day, later in the week," she recently informed me. Then she asked, "How old are you going to be again? 47 or 48? I can't remember."

HURRICANE TALES

The usual Palm Beach salutation, "You look wonderful," (which really means I'll be asking you in private for the plastic surgeon's number) has now been replaced with, "How'd you make out?", (which, of course, refers to the hurricanes 2004, not the divorce settlement.)

HURRICANE FRANCES

As Frances was still spinning away in the open waters of the Caribbean, I was sitting home staring at my e-mail confirmation from Delta Airlines: Leaving West Palm Beach at 6 AM September 1st, connecting in Dallas, arriving in Seattle 12:30 PM. Somebody (probably me), had the ingenious idea to fly out to Seattle to celebrate my son's 21st Birthday with him, provided he wasn't crawling through a sand pit in the Sunni Triangle.

On Monday, two days before my departure, Frances was heading straight for Jacksonville. On Tuesday, the path moved slightly south, still far enough to the north as not to cause much concern. When I arrived in Seattle on Wednesday afternoon, I made a quick call to my wife's boss, Phil Troscolair, a self-professed meteorologist and trivia savant, who said, "It looks like Vero and I'm not worried." With that information at hand, my wife, son and I piled into the rental car and headed west, to the Olympic Peninsula.

We had been dully warned by friends that the Olympic Peninsula was a bit "backward". After experiencing one of the worst salad bars of my life at an eatery in Forks, Washington (one bowl of Iceberg lettuce and six tubs filled with unidentifiable chunks smothered in a mayonnaise based substance), the lack of a cell phone signal or even a phone booth that worked, came as no surprise. As we checked into the Crescent Lodge on our first night we were informed that for some unknown reason the electricity had gone out: there was no food, no ice, no phone service and no hot water available, but the management was willing to shave a few dollars off the quoted rate. For those amenities, we later joked, we could have stayed home.

Throughout the first weekend we had a difficult time garnering any information about the condition of South Florida. Finally, on Monday I reached my buddy Sarge on his cell phone who informed me that there was no need for us to rush back home. "The palm tree laying across your pool isn't going anywhere and the house looks intact." Being the

49

pessimist, I responded, "Sarge, don't sugarcoat it." He then continued, "OK, the chimney blew away, the screens ripped out of your pool house and most of the landscaping is gone." With that information, we decided to take our friend's advice and stay the entire 10 days, then come home.

As we pulled into our driveway late Saturday night, we spotted our neighbors Jackie and Bernice standing outside their home. "You timed it perfectly, the power just came on just a few hours ago," Bernice told us. Jackie then offered his help the next morning getting the palm tree out of the pool.

We all know what cancer survivor Lance Armstrong has accomplished, but let me tell you about Jackie House. Diagnosed with leukemia less than a year ago, the 63 year old native Kentuckian has undergone months of radiation and chemotherapy. Days after returning home from prolonged hospital stays I've witnessed him: trimming 25 foot tall palm trees, digging holes for fence posts, mowing his lawn and pressure cleaning his patio. So it came as no surprise on Sunday morning that Jackie showed up to give us a hand. While my wife and I watched, he took a twelve foot long 4x4 and using it as a fulcrum, slowly edged the palm tree off our pool and then proceeded to cut it up with his chain saw. Standing there in awe of his physical prowess, my wife said to me, "What's the matter with you, can't you at least help him?" Maybe feeling a bit embarrassed for me, Jackie told us, "Don't worry, I've got this under control."

HURRICANE JEANNE

Two weeks after Hurricane Frances, another hurricane loomed off the coast. I'm not sure when it was, exactly, that I dropped the ball, but I noticed that every house in our neighborhood, except ours, had either hurricane shutters or plywood covering its windows. I had a sinking feeling in my stomach. My philosophy up until now was, if the wind is strong enough to blow out the windows, it will blow the roof off as well. This mantra was of little consolation as I sat huddled in our safe room/closet as Hurricane Jeanne unleashed her fury. I promised myself that if I made it out of this storm alive, I would buy hurricane shutters before next year's hurricane season.

My wife, who has a slight hearing impairment due to one Grateful Dead concert too many, and Lou, our 92 year-old friend and evacuee from a mobile home in Hobe Sound, both slept soundly and peacefully throughout the whole night. Me, I pulled an all-nighter. When my wife arose the next morning and noticed I hadn't slept, she asked where I had been all night. Garnishing a two day stubble on my face and feeling moderately disheveled, I replied, "In the spider hole."

TO ADD INSULT TO INJURY

One week after picking up the pieces of Hurricane Jeanne I found myself driving on AIA in Manalapan, taking the slow/scenic route to Boca Raton. Just as I passed the battered Ritz-Carlton tower, a car coming towards me ran off the northbound shoulder, overcorrected and careened head-on towards me. The only evasive action I could take was to steer hard right towards the small swatch of grass between the roadway and the intracoastal. Luckily my car came to rest between a palm tree and the mega-yacht, Octopussy.. I would personally like to thank Duvall's Towing for their prompt and courteous service. As for the driver of the green S-Type Jag, who didn't have the civility to stop, you were in the minority. This hurricane season brought out the best in most people.

THE DAY I NEVER MET JOHN LENNON

My father loved Sunday mornings. He would wake up at the crack of dawn and drive down to the Jersey Bakery. Since we lived in upstate New York, I could never figure out why the owner named it "Jersey"- and a buy a dozen hard rolls and a dozen sticky buns, hot out of the ovens. He then would begin his rounds, visiting his friends for coffee and conversation. My Sunday mornings consisted of watching "The Three Stooges" on TV and beating up on my younger brother, Steve. My father often suggested one of us 'tag along' in an effort to give my mother a few hours of 'peace and quiet', which was just fine by me.

One of the regulars on the Sunday Morning Coffee Clutch was an apple farmer down the road named Gene. I always thought it a bit strange that Gene would dress in knickers and a cardigan sweater and drive around the property on a golf cart. But who was a 12- year-old to criticize a grown man? I would often drive his cart through the orchards pretending I was driving in the Paris-Dakar Road Rally, and it was a miracle I didn't wrap it around the trunk of a Red Delicious apple tree. One day I asked my father, "What's up with Gene's clothes?" He told me that Gene was a professional golfer who had won a lot of tournaments, and that was his preferred attire. The fact that I knew little or nothing about Gene's accomplishments wasn't surprising. I didn't have much interest in golf as a kid. When I was nine years old, I was knocked unconscious by an errant golf ball at a miniature golf course, and developed an aversion to any game that involved a hard white ball. It wasn't until several years later, after Gene and his wife had sold the farm and moved to Marco Island, that I learned what a legend Gene Sarazen was. As Gene would have said, "That was par for the course."

Another regular on my father's Sunday morning sojourns was his friend, Morris. During the week Morris lived in New York City where he ran his record company, Roulette Records. Come Friday afternoon, he would hop into his baby blue Cadillac Eldorado convertible and drive upstate to his fifteen hundred acre dairy farm. In addition to a plethora of farm machinery, Morris owned a garage full of motorized toys including motorcyles, ATV's, and snowmobiles, all of which were at my disposal. During the summer months we were invited to use his Olympic-sized cement pond, which was a real treat. My usual swimming hole was often brimming with snapping turtles, snakes and a hefty sampling of cow manure.

One winter morning I was in our garage rebuilding the carburetor on my minibike when my father came out and asked me if I was interested in taking a ride over to Morris' farm. "He has a houseguest this weekend who was one of the Beatles," he told me. "Nah, I'm too busy working on my engine," I replied. "OK, I'll take your brother with me then," he said.

Later that afternoon when I saw my eight-year-old brother in his room sorting through his baseball card collection, I asked him what he did over at Morris' farm that morning. "Played pool and taught John Lennon how to play ping pong," he answered. He then showed me the autographed note John Lennon had given him. I may have been slightly jealous, but even at an early age I was never that impressed with celebrities.

A short time after my brother's encounter with John, my father's friend Morris released a record containing a "Best Of" collection of John Lennon's songs, which was apparently never authorized by the former Beatle. An ensuing court battle was chronicled in various newspapers, and Morris eventually lost. During a subsequent Sunday excursion to his farm I remember him telling my father, "Of course I lost. The jury sat there watching a pregnant Yoko knitting a %^$@ baby sweater the whole time!"

During the late 1970's Lennon and his family made several trips to Palm Beach, often staying at the Colony Hotel. As photographer Lucien Capehart was quoted saying to a People Magazine reporter, "John loved Palm Beach, everyone here left him alone."

In January of 1980 Lennon and his wife Yoko Ono bought Brownie McLean's former South Ocean Boulevard estate, El Salano, for $725,000. A complete restoration immediately began, but Lennon never returned to see the mansion finished.

In a recent conversation, my brother, Steve, informed me that he had given his personalized John Lennon autograph to his best friend not long after receiving it. And, ironically, he too was just writing a short story about that eventful day. His version of the events was fictionalized, but we both were in agreement with the basic facts. Regretfully, his documentation that his friend's grandmother threw that autograph in the garbage was true.

Another tidbit of Beatle trivia is that John Lennon while vacationing in Palm Beach wrote the song, "Serve Yourself". For those in town who might have been offended by the suggestion that 'the help' have a day off, it was later revealed in a book by author Robert Rosen that the song was actually a parody of Bob Dylan's song, "You Gotta Serve Somebody."

In 1986, one of my first photo assignments for the Palm Beach Daily News was to photograph a home at 720 South Ocean Boulevard. Court records had recently indicated that Yoko Ono had sold the property to a Boston family for 3.15 million dollars.

This Wednesday, December 8th, 2004, marks the 24th anniversary of Lennon's death.

IN HARM'S WAY

Each night after dinner, my father would walk into the den, turn on the TV, sit back in his well worn recliner, light up his 100th Lucky Strike cigarette of the day, and watch the Huntley-Brinkley report. Back in those days the news usually began with reports from Viet Nam..... body counts, massacres and battles for hills designated only by numbers. All this had been bad enough to watch when we had a small black and white television, but my father saw to it that we had the first color TV on the block. Now we could watch all the mayhem of war in living color.

I knew my father had served in the Navy during World War II because one day I discovered a box packed away in the garage. In it were various photos, a box of colored bars and pins, and a framed Honorable Discharge certificate. He never once spoke of his military service or made any comments about the Viet Nam War. That was, until he got a call one night from his older sister, Millie, who lived in Trenton.

Apparently my older cousin, Stanley, who had just graduated from college, had the unfortunate luck to have an extremely low number in the draft lottery. As not to postpone the inevitable, he decided he would enlist in the Army. I'm not sure I actually saw smoke emanating from my father's ears when he heard all of this, but my mother rushed in from the kitchen and yelled, as she often did, "Calm down before you give yourself a heart-attack!" Amazingly, it was not for another 20 years before my father did indeed give himself his first cardiac arrest.

My cousin did enlist, but in the National Guard. As he also had a teaching certificate (teachers were then exempt from the draft), he soon moved into my grandmother's old farmhouse and started a new job as a social studies teacher in our county school system. The arrangement was he would eat dinner with our family on Tuesday, Thursday and Sunday nights.

On the evenings my cousin ate with us, conversation would start out civilized and in an acceptable volume level, until Stanley brought up the subject of 'the war'. He was dismayed that he wasn't in Viet Nam serving his country and I could see my father's blood pressure slowly start to rise from across the table. Soon he would start screaming, slamming his fists on the formica table, "You want the truth, you can't handle the truth!" (Actually I made that quote up, but it was something to that effect.) Soon, my father and Stanley were one step away from a World Wrestling Federation SmackDown. Strange as it was, I didn't mind it, as my father's attention was now temporarily diverted from his ire about my long hair, horrible report cards and general adolescent langour.

The reason I remembered all this is because my aunt just sent me an envelope containing my father's official Navy portrait, something she thought I should have to pass along to my son. She also suggested I could contact the Department of the Navy to get a copy of his service records and request replacements of the medals he was awarded.

Within the matter of a few weeks I not only received a copy of my father's service records, but was able to put together all the pieces of the puzzle that had eluded me for decades.

My father, having just graduated from high school, enlisted in the Navy on September 6, 1943. After receiving training to become a radioman, he was assigned to the 459-foot troop transport ship, the USS Storm King. I did a 'Google' search for the ship's name and learned that an annual reunion for the crew of the Storm King had recently been held in Henderson, Kentucky.

A local Henderson resident, George Nasbitt, had hosted the event. I easily obtained George's phone number from the directory and soon found myself speaking with the 79 year-old vet. George informed me that a group of fourteen veterans and families attended the latest reunion, "There aren't many of us left anymore." When I asked him if he remembered my father, he wasn't sure. "That was almost 60 years ago, my memory really isn't that good." He did, however, clearly remember all the major engagements the ship was involved in: Saipan, Anguar, Leyete, Iwo Jima, Okinawa, New Guinea, Palau and Luzon, some of which were the fiercest battles in the Pacific. "We were under a constant barrage of kamikaze attacks. Thankfully we never took a direct hit. In Saipan, the tables on the mess deck had to be turned into first aid tables. The sounds from all the injured soldiers were so awful the crew couldn't sleep at night." I was starting to see why my father was so reluctant to reminisce about his war years.... they weren't good memories. George then gave me a few names and telephone numbers of some of the other surviving members of the crew, "Maybe some of them will remember your dad," he then added, "We're having the next reunion in Louisville, if your interested, we'd love to have you attend."

I went down the list: Warren Powell in Ohio, Harold Ausmus in

Kentucky, Joseph Singer in Illinois and finally George Stevens in Virginia. George Stevens had just returned home from a lengthy stay in the hospital, but yes, he did recall my father. "I happen to have a copy of the ship's January 1945 newsletter, and there is a mention of his big feet. I'll send it to you." I did in fact receive a copy of "The Sea Breeze" in the mail a few days later and called George to thank him. A voice on the other end asked me what the nature of my call was, and was then told, "Mr. Stevens passed away last night."

As my father often said, "Enough was enough." I now had a clearer picture of why father's temper was so easily elevated all those evenings at the dinner table. Obviously he didn't want to see his nephew flown home in a flag draped coffin from Viet Nam. Maybe he had also seen the futility and insanity of Viet Nam on TV all those nights. Luckily for me, the last troops were leaving the embassy in Saigon as I graduated from High School and I never had to endure my father's wrath about war. Not that I was that anxious about participating in anything that had the word 'military' attached to it.

I recently spoke with my Aunt Millie, who just turned 83 and still lives in Trenton. "You know," she said, "Your father was 18 when he went off to war, just like your son. At that age they're so naive, they think they can change the world, but it's the world that changes them." Roger that.

DOLLARS AND NO SENSE

For the past year, I've been getting a daily deluge of e-mails from my old buddy, Jim. Most have been political in content, but every once in awhile there is a personal message attached. For example: "Mike, I'm now living in Moscow with my new Russian bride, Masha, and a translator. She doesn't speak English and I don't speak Russian. You can only imagine how much this is costing me!"

According to the DesMoinesRegister.com's Famous Iowans webpage, Jim's grandfather, Roswell Garst, was Iowa's most famous farmer. He was an agricultural pioneer who promoted and sold hybrid corn seed throughout the world and had also become a noted confidant of Nikita Khrushchev. His philosophy was, "Better to feed your enemies than to fight them." After the Russian president paid a visit to the Garst's Coon Rapids, Iowa farm in 1959, Jim's older brother, Sam, appeared with Khrushchev on the cover of LIFE Magazine. What began in 1930 in an Iowa shack, the Garst hybrid corn seed business grew into a company that had over $100,000,000 gross sales and land holdings of over 20,000 acres. This included a fertilizer company and majority ownership in several banks near the time of Roswell's death in 1997. Needless to say, Jim's stock in the Garst Seed Company wasn't chicken feed.

During high school, when I first met Jim, he was every bit 'off the farm.' He would sometimes dress in overalls, flannel shirts, and Dunham work boots, which were usually left unlaced. He also had an incredible collection of music. His albums were stacked neatly in rows alphabetically, encompassing all four walls of the room. And most importantly at that time, Jim's agricultural acumen wasn't only growing corn. His success with another "crop" wasn't left unappreciated by a select group of students, me included.

I lost track of Jim after he went off to college, but every year or so I would get a card from him postmarked Ecuador, Peru or Tierra del Fuego. Jim eventually fell completely off the radar until eight years ago when he called me to say that he was arriving at the airport in West Palm Beach to attend a meeting with a group of investors in Boca Raton. He now owned a gold mine in Nevada and needed some working capital. I offered to pick him up at the airport and then asked how I would recognize him since we hadn't seen each other for almost twenty years. "You can't miss me," was his answer. When I arrived at the airport, true to form, Jim Garst was still larger than life.

Although we had a nice visit, we fell out of touch once again. Then, a few years ago, sitting around with nothing better to do, I called information for Coon Rapids, Iowa and asked if there was any listings for the name, Garst. I was given the number for David, who I remembered was Jim's father.

The first bit of news that Jim's dad related was about Jim's health problems. He was in desperate need of hip replacements and on top of that, he had diabetes. Not to mention he had blown through his entire inheritance, roughly several million dollars. He was now living in a trailer next to his gold mine in Nevada. I was given a number to a hotel where he worked as a night clerk, and I could try to reach him there. Jim answered the phone and we talked for several minutes. I immediately got the gist on just how far down Jim was on his luck. I wished him the best and that was the last time we spoke, until two weeks ago.

How Jim got from the gold mine to Russia I couldn't quite follow, but last week he was back in the United States hoping to recover any money owed to him by investors. He told me he was now penniless, living the past year on credit cards. He added, "A professor once told me the most speculative investments were oil wells, Broadway productions and gold mines." I couldn't help to ask him, "Jim, didn't you work as a financial planner for awhile? Shouldn't you have known better?" "I'm a risk taker," was his answer. He went on, "My sister is sitting on millions, she invested wisely. All it has cost me is $1,000,000, my family, my home, my credit, my career, one third of my life, my emotional well being and my dignity. But I remain optimistic."

As I began to ponder all of this, I placed a to call Doug Regan, Chairman and CEO of Northern Trust Bank of Florida. I told him about my friend Jim, and he responded, "That's not an unfamiliar story. It's almost like a Shakespearean tragedy." I wondered why Jim's grandfather didn't do anything to prevent any of his heirs from being so audacious with his hard earned dollars. He went on to explain, "Estate planning can make people very uncomfortable. Money and mortality are really major issues. It can be very chilling. When children inherit large sums of money," he continued, "the fundamental drive to produce and work towards a goal is taken away." I wasn't sure this explained my friends' exact predicament, but it was comforting to know that neither I, nor my son, would be in need of Doug's services anytime soon.

BACK IN THE SADDLE

For the record, let me emphatically state, I am not, nor have I ever been a doctor. I never attended medical school or college. In fact, I barely passed introduction to biology during my sophomore year in high school. I've never tried to pass myself off as any kind of medical practitioner, healer, or shaman. Yet, whenever any of my friends has a problem with his or her back, I'm the first person they call.

I suppose enduring years of constant lower back pain, crippling muscle spasms and excruciating sciatica make me somewhat of an authority on the matter. Over the past decade I've consulted with neurologists, orthopaedics, chiropractors, masseuses, physical therapists and just about anyone else who would listen to my litany of misery. I have drawers full of x-rays, MRI's and prescription bottles of Flexeril, Lodine, Soma and Percocet. I subjected myself to every known treatment except surgery and a pilgrimage to Lourdes. And now, miraculously it has been three full years since I've experienced any major discomfort in my lower back, not even a twinge. Why am I telling you about this? I guess it may be because I just received a newsletter from a local hospital. The two-inch tall banner headline reads: The "Minimally Invasive" Evolution of Spinal Surgery. Thanks, but no thanks!

One piece of advice I've often heard repeated, from my father-in-law to my mechanic, was, "Surgery is your last resort. When you can no longer walk, or even crawl, then you can think about it." And at one time I was thinking about it. I had suffered three months of sciatica, the worst pain of my life, except for the kidney stone incident at the Mets Spring Training Camp in Port St. Lucie, which is another story. It felt like a pair of scissors was being driven into my legs. I no longer was going out of my mind, I WAS out of my mind. I called the Orthopaedist, and was ready to sign on the dotted line. "Get the IV and gurney ready... STAT!," I told the receptionist.

I never made it out the door, because my friend Stephanie, from Georgia called to ask how I was doing. Sensing my discomfort (the swearing may have given her a clue) she directed me to immediately drop what I was doing, get into my car, and drive up to Savannah, "To see Jim." The Jim she was referring to was her husband, Dr. James

Lindley, one of Savannah's most respected neurologists. His prominence in the medical community I believed, was because of his surgical skills, rather than his charm and good looks. " And don't forget to bring all your films with you," were her closing instructions. Incidentally, the night before I had watched Jim on one of my favorite reality TV shows, "Trauma, Life in the ER." That evening's episode featured the staff from Savannah's Memorial Medical Center. A motorcyclist had an unfortunate encounter with a telephone pole, and Jim was called in to try to piece his brain back together. I was hoping my prognosis wouldn't be as gloomy as the guy with the Harley.

The very next afternoon I arrived at Jim's office, underwent a series of tests, then drove back to the Lindley residence to await the diagnosis. Jim arrived home later that evening with a large take-out container of "Low Country Boil", which is a Southern-style stew containing shrimp, crab, potatoes, sausage and corn, and my MRI films under his arm. Later, as I sat down with his family around the kitchen center island, Jim plunged his fork into the spicy concoction and said, "Mike, there isn't really anything wrong with you. You've got a slight curvature of the spine, the herniation in the lower disk has receded, and you're in good overall health for a guy your age. You need to strengthen the muscles in your abdomen, which in turn will help support your back and spine. I recommend you try yoga." There I was expecting to hear I would need to be splayed open on an operating room table like a Thanksgiving turkey and now I'm told my cure is a regimen of down dogs, happy babies and dead bug positions! And then he added, "If you want to continue playing golf, shorten your backswing."

Needless to say I immediately enrolled in a yoga studio, taking three evening classes per week. Within a month I noticed a marked improvement. I slept better at night and no longer had a constant, nagging lower back pain. After 6 months my friends commented on my overall physical appearance, noting that my posture was better and often asking if I had lost weight. I was not however, mistaken for Brad Pitt. Soon it was over a year without any episodes of back issues or muscle spasms, and I'm now celebrating the start of my fourth year of a "pain-free" back. I make it a point to regularly attend a yoga class, at least twice a week if possible. Which brings me to my most recent consultation.

My friend Susie arrived in Palm Beach on Christmas Eve after a marathon road trip from her home in Martha's Vineyard. She hobbled in complaining of an aching and stiff back. "What should I do Mike?," she asked me. I told her to soak in a hot bath, and don't do anything strenuous for the next few days. The next afternoon she called me from the Don Carter Bowling Lanes. "Mike, I decided to go bowling with my daughter and now I'm laying on Lane 27. My back went totally out, I can't move! What do I do now?" Two months, four doctor visits, one MRI and one cortisone shot later, my friend is starting to feel better. I can only shake my head in bewilderment.

When it comes to back problems, my prescription is common sense and yoga. Do my friends listen? Usually not. When not dispensing my own advice, I often quote another good friend, Hans, who once told me, "Given time, 95% of the medical ailments will heal themselves. The problem is, the other 5% will kill you."

CAT SCRATCH FERVOR

I'm no Catherine Bradley (aka The Cat Lady of Palm Beach), but I've had my fair share of four-legged, furry, feline friends in my life. In fact the newest member of our family, Noodles, has inspired me to finally strip off all the old wallpaper in our hallway. She has graciously spearheaded this long overdue project by scratching away a two foot high section for the length of the corridor, leaving an ample amount of wall space for me to scrape and scrub.

Although my grandmother had several colonies of feral cats on her farm, I was, according to my mother, drawn to the more complacent chickens. She tells the story of how my grandmother would often feed me dinner in the chicken coop because I was so enamored of the poultry. It wasn't until I moved into a farmhouse with four members of a R&B band in upstate New York that I developed a meaningful relationship with a fissiped mammal.

Bowser was a welcome addition to our ramshackle abode, if for no other reason than to keep the mice at bay. One day the piano player, Leo, decided Bowser needed a companion. We drove to the local Humane Society where we acquired a kitten he named Duck. Most of the musicians I have known spend the majority of their day waiting around so they can play a gig at night. Thus, the frisky kitten provided ample amusement for the household, especially when a new visitor was in the house and someone yelled, "DUCK!" Their usual reaction was to bend over and to put their arms protectively over their head, perhaps expecting a golf ball to come flying through the window. Eventually the band disbanded, and Leo and I shared joint custody of the cats.

Not long after starting graduate school, my wife returned to our home with a new orange tabby, named Sunny. For some unfortunate reason, Sunny wondered off to a nearby field, where his leg was snared in a furrier's trap. The vet assured me a cat would adjust very nicely to only three legs, and of course I resisted all attempts to rename him Tripod.

I'm not sure what prompted me to consider delving into the world of a cat fancier, but soon a Brown Burmese kitten named Mao was prancing around the house. A few months after Mao arrived we welcomed another member of our family, a son. For some unknown reason our newborn refused to sleep in the crib my mother had bought for us, but it suited the cat just fine. My mother, even to this day, still chides me, "I paid $300 for a Maple crib that only the cat slept in." The Burmese breed is supposedly noted for its extreme intelligence, but Mao was intent on traveling far out of his way to find a road, where he met his demise.

Mao's replacement was yet another Brown Burmese, who, my now two-year old son, named Bobby-Chin. I didn't know what it was with these cats, but Bobby, too, had a death wish and was buried not far from where he was squished by a passing car. It was exactly at that point I said to my wife, "Enough with these expensive cats."

Upon moving to Florida, our next cat, Mittens, was inherited from her elderly owners, whose house we purchased in El Cid. Apparently, Mittens was just as along in years as her former guardians, and we provided a peaceful resting place in our new backyard next to the grapefruit tree.

Mitten's replacement, Baba, wandered in from the infamous Proctor's Restaurant cat colony. It was no secret that the cats living near the Dixie Highway landmark feasted daily on a delectable array of leftovers, so why this cat in particular decided to test the waters elsewhere, was anyone's guess. Baba moved with us to North Palm Beach, where he lived out his years in our backyard, supplementing his diet of Friskies with lizards, squirrels, and toads.

As it had been almost two years without the patter of little paws in the house, my son, who was home visiting at Thanksgiving, suggested we procure another "friend" for his mother, as a birthday present. We arrived at the Peggy Adams Animal Rescue League, overwhelmed by over one hundred adoptable cats. My son began to scrutinize and hold each and every cat before making his decision. I wandered around reading the cards attached to each cage: Won't use litterbox; Doesn't like children; Only eats poached salmon, etc. It appeared every cat had some sort of 'issue'. What seemed like hours later, my son called out, "Dad, I found mom's cat." I went over to where he was standing holding a cute calico in his arms, and attached to the cage was a card that read: Female Stray, neutered, approximately 2 years old. I asked the attendant what exactly that meant, and she informed me, "Probably a cat that was lost in the hurricane." As for a name, my son determined Noodles fit her just fine.

After I finish with removing the wallpaper and repairing the plaster, I've already got my next project in sight..... repainting the wicker couch which 'somebody' has used instead of her scratching post, which sits nearby.

SOUR GRAPES

I just saw the Academy Award nominated film "Sideways", a quirky (by Hollywood standards) story about two friends who spend a week together touring the wine region of California. It was then I realized that everything I know about fine wines I learned in my senior year of high school. And sad to say, I haven't gained much oenophilic knowledge since.

My last year of secondary education was spent at the Northfield Mt. Hermon School. This institution, historically steeped in religious and moral values, is situated alongside the bucolic shores of the Connecticut River in Northwestern Massachusetts. My academic skills were "marginal" and my athletic acumen was nil, unless you credited my frequent forty mile round-trip bicycle excursions to the liquor store in Brattleboro, Vermont as a phys-ed elective. And for the record, I was of legal drinking age by State government standards, but the school tried, of course, to enforce a 'no alcohol on campus' policy.

My wine cellar, or bureau drawer as it was, contained primarily domestic labels: Boone's Farm, Richard's Irish Rose or Ripple. Occasionally I would branch out into a fine import; Mateus or Blue Nun Liebfraumilch. It was in fact a bottle of the latter that earned me my first three day suspension. In celebration of my best friend Jon's eighteenth birthday, we uncorked an ice cold bottle of '73 Blue Nun, only to be immediately busted by the school security officer. Unbeknownst to us, we had been placed under surveillance due to our questionable and frequent hikes into the woods. As we sat in the Dean of Students office, Jon was asked to call his mother and inform her of his 'unscheduled holiday.' Since this was the evening of his birthday, his mother told him, "Just because you're eighteen, that doesn't mean you're a man." Last week I helped Jon celebrate his 50th birthday at his mother's Palm Beach home. As I've done each year on his birthday, for the past 32 years, I said, "Jon, just because you're (50), that doesn't mean you're a man." His mother, who remembered that fateful night, laughed along with us.

Several years ago I was asked by a gentlemen who was celebrating the sale of his NFL franchise team to photographically document the eight course dinner he was arranging at Amici Restaurant for his family and a select group of friends. He also noted that he was flying in a world renowned sommelier from France who would help host this event. Between each course I was relegated back to the bar in front of the restaurant. As the evening wore on, the 'regulars' sitting at the bar became more and more interested in what was transpiring, both gastronomically and libatiously. I reported to my newly formed inquisitive friends: "The last course was an organically raised hand-fed Belgium grouse stuffed with Madagascar fennel and Normandy shallots braised in an Iberian truffle juice and was served with a Chateau Lafite Rothschild. This isn't the kind of dinner you can order in a drive-thru," I added. They respectfully nodded their heads in agreement. As the night wore on into the wee hours, a waiter emerged and announced, "Mr. C would like you to have a glass of Chateau-Mouton Rothschild Pauillac 1945." Truth be told, he could have said it was a 1996 Vintage Welch's Grape Juice and I would have been just as impressed. I glanced in both directions down the bar, all heads were staring at the glass placed before me. "Who would like a swig?" I invited. The glass then made its way, passing from hand to hand, each person taking time to inhale the aroma before taking a sip. I've always said, "When in Rome......." so as I now was ready to partake in what had become a hedonistic (by Palm Beach standards) ritual I lifted the glass and announced, "I hope nobody here has festering cold."

I don't have a subscription to The Wine Spectator (I do, however, have a subscription to Popular Mechanics). I don't even bother to read the wine list at restaurants anymore, pretending to know what I should be looking for. I just hand over the leather bound encyclopedia to my wife. As for myself, I usually inquire about a pale, dry, recent vintage ginger ale. The familiar response being, "Would a Canada Dry 2005 be acceptable, sir?"

WHAT WERE THE
"ODDS AGAINST TOMORROW"?

Back in August of 1957, long before air-conditioned multiplex cinemas and satellite televison, entertainment in small town America was hard to come by. Except, that was, if you lived in a particular small town in upstate New York. My parents, along with a few hundred others, crammed the brightly lit main drag each night, hoping to catch a glimpse of a real movie star. That was known as 'The Summer Hollywood Came to Hudson'.

Reviewed as a "Crackling crime caper with an undercurrent of racial tension, combining the desperation of three men, two of whom hate each other, and the culmination of that desperation being a bank robbery," 'Odds Against Tomorrow' is considered by many film critics to be a film noir gem. The film stars Harry Belafonte, Robert Ryan, Ed Begley and Shelly Winters as small time New York City criminals trying to make a big score at a rural bank 'up in the sticks'. As fate would have it, my father's modest accounting business was located adjacent to the bank, and he was asked if Harry Belafonte could use the office for a dressing room. As most of the filming was done at night, my father would still be able to work uninterrupted during the day. As for compensation from the production company, I think the personally signed album, 'Belafonte Sings The Caribbean' was it.

After the film had wrapped, Belafonte had become so enamored with the area he decided to buy a small estate in Chatham, New York, just a few miles up the road from the movie location. At the end of his driveway hung a sign, 'Day-O Farm'. As another point of trivia, the Three Stooges (brothers Moe, Shemp and Curly Howard) had previously lived and worked on a nearby family farm, albeit forty-five years before the Belafonte's arrival. This staid, bucolic community two hours north of Manhattan is primarily known for Sunday morning fox hunts and its Shaker Museum. It was a well known fact that newcomers, locally referred to as carpetbaggers, weren't always welcomed with open arms.

During the late 60's I remember seeing our local newspaper with a front page headline: "Harry Belafonte Arrested For Shoplifting." My recollection was that Mr. Belafonte had been apprehended leaving the local A&P grocery store without paying for a loaf of bread. His explanation was his elderly mother had taken ill and he was rushing with her to seek medical attention. The story played out for months, and I assumed charges were eventually dropped. I didn't think about this incident often, but occasionally I would cross paths with Mr. Belafonte at our local Asian Take-Out, The Pacific Trader. I would nod in recognition as he picked up his to-go order and watch as he swiftly exited, his car left running in the parking lot.

I thought about the motivations behind his arrest and subsequent public humiliation, which unfortunately alienated him from the community. Other well-known residents, such as jazz singer Mabel Mercer occasionally held concerts to help benefit the local humane society. Media mogul Rupert Murdoch, who owned a secluded weekend retreat in the area, held a screening of Gallipoli (his own production) at the local movie theater to benefit the historical society. There was also a host of other famous 'locals' doing their part to help the volunteer fire department, the hospital or a favorite charity. I noted Harry Belafonte never stepped forth, and it didn't take much to wonder why.

To make sure I had a clear picture of the those turn of events, I contacted the weekly newspaper in Chatham, New York, The Chatham Courier. A woman who identified herself as Alice Davis, the office manager, told me she was a life long resident of the area and did remember the 'incident' at the A&P almost 40 years ago. "I think it was blown out of proportion, and unfortunately the store manager overreacted." I then asked her if she thought it was racially motivated, mentioning to her that Harry Belafonte had been a figure at the forefront of the civil rights movement at the time. "No way in hell," was her answer. "There were a few other minor problems with his kids in regard to inattentive driving, but nothing that drastic. And as far as that loaf of bread, I thought it was a toothbrush, and the woman with him was his mother-in-law." Inquiring if she had seen 'Odds Against Tomorrow', Alice's opinion was, "It wasn't 'Gone With The Wind', but it was good."

Harry Belafonte made an appearance in Palm Beach back in 1993 to benefit the National Wheelchair Sports Fund. The event was held at the Royal Poinciana Playhouse, and Jesse Newman had asked me to come backstage to photograph Mr. Belafonte along with some of the organization's prime supporters. During a lull in the offstage activities, I mentioned to Mr. Belafonte that I had previously lived in the Chatham area and would often spot him at The Pacific Trader. He gave me an acknowledging grin, then turned to walk on stage to a sold-out house, his fans anxiously awaiting his arrival.

Today Belafonte donates most of his time and energy to charitable and philanthropic efforts. He serves as a Goodwill Ambassador for UNICEF and is the recipient of the Peace Corps Leader for Peace Award. He also donates twenty percent of his income to the Belafonte Foundation of Music and Art, which helps African-American students study for careers in the arts. He recently received a Grammy Award for Lifetime Achievement and a National Medal of Arts. As for walking out of stores without paying for toothbrushes, I haven't noticed any of those headlines lately.

MISTAKEN IDENTITY

Where I came from, many of us had nicknames. They were either derived from one's physical attributes: Boxhead Hills (cranium), Hook LaValley (nose), Uncle Popeye Keil (thyroid condition) and Smellvin' Melvin (personal hygiene). Others were more reflective of one's character: "Dubious" Gallo, "Nature" Wurster and "Mad Dog" Lacetti all come to mind. Even my little brother, Steve, who had an unfortunate encounter with a fire hydrant while riding his bicycle, was forever nicknamed "Scar," which was in fact shortened from "Scarface."

And then there were the nicknames whose origins made no sense whatsoever: We referred to Paul as Felix, Jerry as Manfred, and Brian as Plooker. One of my high school girlfriends, Meredith, preferred to be addressed as Meredy. After graduation, she legally changed her name to Tiffany and then asked to be called Tiff. This all became so confusing to me that ultimately I decided to pursue a relationship with someone else, preferably somebody that kept to one name. As for myself, just "Mike" seemed to work out for the best.

When we first moved to West Palm Beach in the 1980s, I would often get calls for Mike Price, the welder. More disconcerting were the calls in the middle of the night asking for Debbie Price, the public defender who bore the same name as my wife. Sorry, I would inform the caller who was most likely standing in front of a pay phone at the county stockade, this Debbie only works with plants.

I began thinking about all this because I recently received a multitude of phone calls, from both acquaintances and strangers, congratulating me on my $25 million donation to the Albert Einstein College of Medicine. After several minutes of misplaced accolades, I had to sadly inform the caller that the person they really wanted to congratulate was "the other Michael Price," the Palm Beach philanthropist. And for the record, I did just buy a raffle ticket benefitting a children's cancer center in Tampa . . . for $2.

I have often toyed with the idea of producing a photographic essay on those with my name. I've been told that there is a Michael Price who is the artistic director of the Goodspeed Opera House in Haddam, Conn. Then there was a Mike Price with whom I traded correspondence , the music critic for the Houston Chronicle. One year at a polo match in Wellington, I encountered a Michael Price whose business card stated he was the Press Secretary for the British Embassy. He had the proper accent, so I believed him. There was also the Michael Price who was the football coach for Alabama. He was fired for inappropriate behavior, which reportedly included spending too much time at a strip club and alleged antics in a hotel room with two women. Coach Price has denied the latter charges. I got my share of phone calls ribbing me on that one.

Last week I was writing a check for materials I purchased at General Sheet Metal in Riviera Beach when Lynn, the office manager, looked up and said, "Hey, I know another Mike Price; he's a welder in Lake Park." I asked her to write down his phone number and address for me. I was anxious to speak with the man whose phone calls I received all those years ago.

Located in an industrial park off Old Dixie Highway in Lake Park, Welding Unlimited is owned by 47-year-old West Palm Beach native Michael Price. A former Pratt-Whitney employee, Price started his welding business 16 years ago. "I like working with my hands; it gives me a lot of satisfaction." I asked him if he had received any phone calls lately congratulating him on his philanthropic efforts. "No, that would be rare," he said. Nor does he remember getting any calls asking for Michael Price, the photographer. He mentioned to me that he does get over to Palm Beach every once in awhile when an unusual job comes up, but he has never heard of "the other Michael Price," either.

I once received a call from the executive assistant to a high-profile CEO in New York City confirming my luncheon meeting at the Four Seasons for that very afternoon. I explained I was in Palm Beach, and unless there was a private jet ready to take me to New York, I wouldn't make that meeting. After a few moments of silence from the other end of the line, I suggested she flip the Rolodex one more card and see if there was another Michael Price. It was as I thought. "That's the one you want to call," I told her. "And if Ron wants to meet ME for lunch when he's back in Palm Beach, I'd love to take him to the 'Four Brothers Pizzeria' in Lake Worth." The offer is still on. I'm in the book.

THE AMAZINGLY ZANY ZEEMANS
AND THEIR Z-WAGONS

If you happened to have been in the metropolitan New York City area in 1973, you may have noticed a family driving around in a Ford LTD Country Squire station wagon painted coral pink with a Vermont vanity license plate: JJZ. You may have also noted that there wasn't one piece of sheet metal on the car that wasn't dented, scratched, scraped or missing. Even the hood was peeled back toward the windshield like the top of a sardine can.

Make no mistake, those were the Zeemans. The car's nickname was "The Waffle." As for the coral pink paint job, I'll take half the responsibility.

The summer after graduating high school, I was working on a dairy farm in Erie County, N.Y. My partner in crime and classmate was Jonathan Huibert Zeeman IV, known to his peers as Hubie. His mother, Joan Javits Zeeman, had generously lent the family station wagon to her son so he could drive from Larchmont, in Westchester County, to his summer employment almost 500 miles away.

On a scorching July afternoon, Hubie and I were in the local hardware store when we spotted a box of coral pink spray paint with a sign indicating that all 12 cans were drastically reduced to $1 per can.

Coral pink obviously wasn't in big demand in farm country. However, having been labeled "doesn't always follow the rules to the detriment of others and themselves" by our guidance counselor, we immediately purchased the case of paint. Neither of us needed to say a word; we knew that the brown station wagon parked outside would soon be a new color.

As ridiculous as we looked driving around in a coral pink station wagon that summer, we could only imagine the stares that Hubie's parents would get while cruising the streets of tony Larchmont. After we returned the station wagon home to his parents, I received a call from my co-conspirator telling me, "My mother loves the new color!"

Joan recently reminded me that two years after abandoning "The Waffle" in a junkyard in Ithaca, N.Y., her son decided to see if it was still intact. Hubie returned to the salvage yard, spotted the car, opened what was left of the door, found the key in the ignition and, amazingly, was able to start the car. He was ready to drive this prototype Z-Wagon away, but all four wheels had rusted off.

A year later, in 1974, I found myself in another Z-Wagon, driving from San Francisco to Yosemite National Park. Packed into the recently acquired but not yet dented vehicle were my buddy Hubie; his girlfriend, Abby; Ande Zeeman, Hubie's younger sister; and her boyfriend Dirk, who also happened to be Donna Reed's nephew. Also in the car was a hitchhiker named Clem whom we picked up along the way.

One evening we stopped at a store along a deserted stretch of road to buy dinner. As we gathered around the station wagon after making our purchases, Clem proudly announced that he had decided to "steal a couple of steaks." We conferred then and there: Clem had to go. As Ken Kesey would have said, "He's off the bus." My last vision of Clem is him standing abandoned alongside the road, the sun setting behind him, not another person for miles. His last vision of us was the back of a Ford LTD station wagon with a bumper sticker on the rear window: "For God and Country." Clem, if you're in prison and reading this, no hard feelings.

My first road trip to Florida was courtesy of yet another Z-Wagon. This time I felt like a modern-day Tom Joad in "The Grapes of Wrath". The car was packed to the brim with an assortment of pets, furniture, appliances, musical instruments and food containers. On the roof rack were bicycles, suitcases and, you guessed it, a kitchen sink.

In an effort to make the journey as fast as possible, driving was divided among Joan, Hubie and me. Somewhere near the North Carolina-South Carolina border I relinquished the driver's seat to Joan. We decided that she would drive until sunrise. I couldn't say how many hours had passed, but I was suddenly awoken by the jolting of the car. As we lurched to a halt, I picked myself up off the back seat and looked out the window. We were in the middle of a cornfield somewhere in Georgia, nowhere near I-95. There never was an explanation of how we ended up there.

A simple trip on I-95 often became an episode from the Twilight Zone, with adventures that included sitting in a stranger's driveway in Macon, coasting on fumes into Pedro's South of the Border at 3 a.m., and losing wardrobes from an opened suitcase on the roof rack.

In what can be described only as an ironic twist of fate, several years later, Joan's mother, Lily, decided to redo the kitchen in her North End home. Leaving the various color choices with the painter, she departed for the summer, hoping to return in time for Christmas to a newly renovated and painted kitchen. Much to her, and everyone else's surprise, the entire kitchen was now painted a shockingly familiar coral pink. Apparently the painter had misread the color code for the paint, or was colorblind. In either case, it was decided that the pink would stay. It continues to this day to be an unforgettable decorating statement.

The Zeeman cars and journeys are only the tip of the iceberg. As the saying goes, "To know them is to love them." In spite of, or because of that infamous paint job, I became the unofficial adopted son of Hans and Joan Zeeman - with a new name: "Priceless." As for the station wagons, signaling a sign of the times, they were eventually replaced by minivans. The license plates also evolved, from Z-WGN to 7-ZEE's to ZLADY to GRANZ. The one thing that hasn't changed after all these years are the zany Zeemans.

THUMBS UP

Over the past several months I've occasionally noticed a distinguished looking, dapperly dressed older gentleman standing on the southbound ramp of I-95 at Northlake Boulevard. Next to him is a green duffel bag with a golf logo embroidered on the side. He has his thumb out, hoping to hitch a ride. Within the few seconds I have to mull over the decision - should I pick him up or not - I've already passed by, flying down the merge lane. If there was ever an innocent, harmless looking hitchhiker to be found in South Florida, he would be the one. Of course, my second thought is, "He may have a gun or machete in that bag."

I had thumbed plenty of rides in my younger, carefree and unwise days. Fortunately, I don't have one of those harrowing tales to tell while reminiscing about 'Back in the Day'. I can note that Carly Simon once stopped to give me a ride in Martha's Vineyard. And the last time, a decade or two ago, I found myself trying to hitch a ride to Vineyard Haven from Edgartown, a young lady driving a well worn Plymouth Valiant informed me she was an editor of a literary magazine for prison inmates. During our brief conversation she told me that her insight into the minds of incarcerated men would prevent her from ever hitch hiking. When I asked why she wasn't hesitant about giving me a lift, she said, "Maybe I had a lapse of judgment, but there isn't a history of serial killers on the Vineyard." When I reached my destination, I thanked her for the ride AND the vote of confidence.

My only real 'memorable' hitchhiking experience was the time I tried to go from northern Maine, back to Albany, New York. A reasonable premise, but what I hadn't accounted for were the notorious black flies. As I stepped out onto the highway, I instantly became a human gummy bear for every known species of blood sucking insect in the Maine wilderness. Eventually, with a series of short rides, I made it to Bangor, where I then stood on the interstate with a sign that read: BOSTON. I was also covered in large, red, welts, which may have given me the 'sympathy' factor I needed to get to Beantown.

Twelve hours after I started my misguided sojourn, I was standing on the Mass Pike entrance in downtown Boston. Home was only a few short hours away. I tried to make eye contact with the drivers as they whizzed pass, hoping that I could generate some sort of aura, like I was a saint sent down from heaven to breathe carbon monoxide fumes until someone rescued my soul. As my hallucinations continued, I thought I recognized an old high school classmate, Bonnie, drive by. I ran after the car towards the toll plaza, frantically waving my hands, hoping she would recognize me as well. Sure enough, it was she and her sister! They welcomed me into the back seat, where I collapsed in the cool, refreshing, air-conditioned comfort. We spoke for a few minutes, and then, relishing my good fortune, I passed out from exhaustion. When I woke up, I assumed an hour or two had passed and I would be seeing signs indicating the New York border was not far ahead. To my dismay, the sign I saw read: Bangor 100 Miles. It had never occurred to me that Bonnie and her sister wouldn't be headed home to upstate New York. They were, in fact, going to Bar Harbor on vacation, and I was almost back to where I started, fifteen hours earlier. I would have laughed, if I had any energy left. I reluctantly asked Bonnie to let me out at the next exit, where I would stand in the fading summer light, hoping to get a ride back to Boston. Luckily I still had the sign.

As it was now pitch black, I thought my chances were very slim for anyone stopping for me, when a couple driving a van stopped. Over the course of the first hour I reiterated to them my life for the past twenty-four hours. They told me they were on their way back to Ohio from a vacation in Maine, and would drive until they were tired, and then would pull off to find a campground for the night. As we neared Boston, they told me that since they really didn't have a set schedule, they would keep driving, and if I gave them directions, they would give me a ride to my front door. They also offered me some Neosporum cream for the insect bites.

I will go out on a limb and say hitchhiking was never popular in Palm Beach. I did, however, have the chutzpah to try to thumb a ride one night from E.R. Bradley's Saloon to the north end of the Island. It was 2 A.M. and I somehow found myself without a ride home. I walked out onto the street and decided to try my luck. Of course traffic was nil, and I pondered the question of who would actually stop to give me a ride at that hour. I soon had my answer: A Palm Beach Police Officer. And the ride, if I wanted one, wouldn't be home. It would be back to the mid-town police station. Weighing my options, I chose the quiet, leisurely, three mile stroll home.

As Jack Kerouac wrote in the quintessential hitchhiking novel, 'On The Road', "One of the biggest troubles with hitchhiking is talking to innumerable people, make them feel like they didn't make a mistake picking you up." I knew the feeling.

ROAD BURN

Just the thought of a road trip makes me car sick, and regretfully, I have both my parents to blame. To this day, I still have nightmares about making the monthly, three hour trek from upstate New York to Trenton, New Jersey. Since my mother was born in Trenton, all of her relatives, including her brother, still resided there. As for my father, as luck would have it, his older sister, Millie, had met and married a man from Trenton, so she too lived there. In short, we traveled from a small, depressing city to a much larger, depressing city to visit our relatives. You may ask yourself why this journey was so traumatic, so I must tell you that both my parents were chain smokers. The combination of cigarette smoke, heat in the summer months, horrible music on the radio and the din of the New York State Thruway was enough to make me want to jump out of my skin AND the car. Mercifully my baby brother, Steve, couldn't verbally complain: he just cried the whole way.

Not long after I turned sixteen and got my driver's license, my father, who had now cut-down to three packs of Lucky Strikes a day, asked me if I would like to take a 'spin' with him in his new Thunderbird. Seven hours later we pulled into the parking lot of L.L. Bean in Freeport, Maine. My father then offered to buy me a new pair of boots, which I suppose was to justify such an absurd, lengthy journey. We bought lobster rolls for dinner, then drove straight back home. When we finally pulled in our driveway, I noted to my father that our 'spin' had only taken 15 hours. I don't remember what his response was, but rest assured he 'lit up' to commemorate our safe arrival.

I did make a series of cross country sojourns in my younger days with non-smoking traveling companions and a box of Dramamine. I also had discovered "The Drive-A-Way Car" method of travel- being able to drive cross-country in someone else's brand new Cadillac or Lincoln Town Car. I'm not sure how popular this arrangement is today, but 'Back In The Day' most newspapers carried an advertisement looking for drivers. Someone would need their car delivered from New York to San Francisco, and the only expense for the driver was gas. If the car was big enough, it could also serve as a hotel room, saving a few extra dollars. You were given a generous time frame, say, eight days to make the journey, and deliver the car to its owner. The trick was to make the trip in three days, so you could then have a car to drive around California for the five extra days. I had perfected this plan by making an arrangement to pick up the next car before the current vehicle was delivered, thus insuring I was never without transportation, or a back seat to sleep in.

My buddy Butch, a self-professed 'Road Scholar', estimates he has logged almost 400,000 miles on the odometer in the course of his thirty-five years as an original member of the Allman Brothers Band. Most of those miles were spent sleeping in a touring bus, more commonly referred to today as a 'land yacht'. During a recent dinner celebrating his birthday, the percussionist recounted to me one of his more memorable highway excursions. "During the late '70's, the band was playing in London and we had a ten day break. I was dating my wife, Melinda at the time, so I hired a Daimler limo with a chauffeur and told him to take us to the best place he knew of, anywhere in Europe. We ferried across the English Channel, then went non-stop (expect for gas and certain beverage refills) through France and Germany until we arrived what may have been a day or two later at a magical village in the middle of the Swiss Alps. We stayed in a castle that was a 5-Star hotel, where we ate, drank and slept in compete bliss. We may have even walked outside once or twice for a hike. Seven days later I had the chauffeur drive us to Zurich, where we caught a plane back to Boston." When I commented about such extravagance, he replied, "The bill for the last dinner alone was almost $2000., but that included 5 bottles of Dom Perignon, which at the time I thought was compliments of the hotel." The Trucks' family has returned to Europe many times over the years for vacations, more likely than not renting a Renault sedan, with Butch at the wheel.

Today, my road trip limit is about six hours, which is just enough to make it to Savannah or Key West without too many aching bones. Ironically, as you are reading this article, I will be returning from Fort Benning, Georgia, an arduous, nine hour drive back to Palm Beach. We were there visiting our son, who the Army decided to send to Fort Benning from Seattle for advanced training exercises. Although this is three hours over my limit, we were happy to make the journey to see him graduate from Ranger School. As the Grateful Dead sing, "What a long strange trip it's been."

BIKE DREAMS

I don't know exactly when my love affair with the bicycle began, but surprisingly it didn't end when I left most of my front teeth and several layers of skin from my face and hands embedded in the asphalt on Oakdale Hill.

For my 10th birthday, my grandmother had given me a shiny new red Stingray bicycle, and of course I couldn't wait to go tearing off on my new ride. The only minor problem was that the bicycle shop neglected to tighten the crucial bolt that held the handlebars in the upright position. Much to the dismay of my parents, years of reconstructive and dental surgeries did little to quench my thirst for two-wheeled adventures. As for the remainder of my adolescence, I survived with only minor abrasions and haematomas.

When most of my high school classmates were cruising around in Pontiac Bonnevilles, Plymouth Belvederes or Chevy Impalas, my preferred mode of transportation was a classic, black, English made Raleigh 3-speed. During the summer months I would start my day by pedaling off to summer school, then to my job washing cars at Milroy Chevrolet. Then, after dinner I would make the three mile trek downtown to meet up with friends at Melino's Bar & Grill.

On one such night after excessive consumption of various libations, I hopped on my trusty steed and headed home. For some unknown reason it occurred to me that if I placed both my feet on either side of the front wheel, I wouldn't need to use the brakes to slow down. I don't remember how many somersaults the bike and I made, but when I finally landed in the middle of the road, a passing car missed crushing my head by inches. Right there and then I swore I would never, ever again use my feet for brakes.

After finally graduating from high school I was able to continue to use the bicycle as my primary form of transportation, thanks in part to a series of menial, low paying jobs. This meant I arrived at work most mornings smelling like the south end of a north bound goat, but nobody seem to notice, or even care. Eventually, I saved enough money to buy a new bicycle, and on the advice of my friend Rob, bought an American made Trek. I picked up my new bicycle on an August afternoon and promptly rode over to Rob's. I carefully balanced the cobalt blue mechanical masterpiece against the side of his car and walked into his house. The only problem was, his wife Cindy, who was walking out the side door, jumped into the car and not noticing my bike, backed over it.

When I later moved to Florida I happily discovered that I could ride my bicycle year-round. In fact, I rode a bicycle to my first job interview at the Shiny Sheet, arriving a bit disheveled. Kim Sargent, then head of the photography department, later told publisher Agnes Ash, "I never saw anyone wearing clothes so wrinkled, but maybe we should hire him anyway." He neglected to mention the ripe body odor.

Four years ago, I fulfilled a dream by embarking on a two-week self-contained bicycle tour of France's Loire Valley. On the Internet I found Claude Blanchard, a former pilot who now rents Puegeot bicycles from his barn outside the city of Angers. Outfitted with hybrid style bicycles, panniers for carrying clothing and supplies, and what looked like a lifetime supply of Michelin maps, my son and I pedaled off on a 300 mile adventure. There would be days when fewer than a half-dozen cars would pass us on picturesque country lanes. One afternoon a car pulled alongside us and the driver leaned over and inquired, "Americans?" I nodded my head and then heard (in French) what I assumed didn't mean, "You must stop at the auberge in the next village and try the foie gras." How I knew this, was by the one fingered salute that followed him steering his car into our path. I tried not to take this random act of French hospitality too personally. When I mentioned this incident to our host, Claude, he apologized, then asked me, "Weren't several tourists killed in Miami when they took a wrong turn out of the airport?"

Today I continue to risk my life by riding my Litespeed Blue Ridge along A1A to Johnny G's or The Dune Dog Café. Last week a green, late model Ford F-150 pickup with a "In Memory of Dale Earnhardt" decal on the rear window pulled alongside me, and the driver yelled out, "Get the %$@*# off the road and onto the sidewalk." Now for the record let me state I'm one who believes the word, sidewalk, should be taken literally. For the benefit of this above-mentioned courteous citizen and others who may not know this, the sidewalk is for people who are walking. Bicycles in the state of Florida have the same rights as motor vehicles, and are expected to share the roadways, not the sidewalks. If you don't like this, don't blame the bicyclists. Blame the residents who insist on fighting the addition of a bike lane along A1A. As for myself, I'm no Lance Armstrong. I often recall the parting words of my friend Claude back in France, "It's not about the destination, it's about the journey."

C'est La Vie.

ROOMS WITHOUT A VIEW.....
OR WINDOW

I'm not sure what I was doing in Jackson Hole, Wyoming last month. I hate the cold weather and haven't seen snow or skied for over twenty years. But there I was, all bundled up in my borrowed ski parka in front of my authentic, rustic, log cabin in Cowboy Village.

When I first realized I would need a place to sleep in Jackson Hole that wouldn't cost several mortgage payments, I called my friend Robert's daughter, who has lived and worked in Jackson Hole for five years. When I asked her to recommend a 'reasonablely priced' accommodation, she informed me, "I know of a bar that has rooms upstairs for $15 a night." I reminded her that I stayed in enough $15 a night rooms in my lifetime, and at my advanced age and refined taste, I required something with more amenities, like a bed and bathroom. "Try Cowboy Village," she replied. "I think they have a website." Sure enough, Cowboy Village did have a website, and when I checked the rates, starting at around $69 per night, I thought I'd better call to make sure there wasn't a mistake. Sure enough, the manager informed me, those were the older summer rates. The winter rates were in fact a few dollars cheaper, and it also included breakfast.

Soon after returning from Jackson Hole I ran into friends who had spent their Christmas vacation in Aspen. They inquired about our stay in Cowboy Village, as they had been skeptical when I originally informed them of the rates. "Yes, there was a bathroom, heat, comfortable beds and a kitchenette.... it couldn't have been better," I told them. As they silently calculated a week's stay at "The Village" as opposed to their slope-side condo in Aspen, Joan pronounced, "That's where we're sending our kids next year!"

During a brief period in my life (1974-1988), I prided myself on finding cheap accommodations. Lisbon: $7 per night, hot water, if any water at all, an additional $2. Belize City: $5 per night, bed bugs and morning rooster symphony, no extra charge. Madrid: $10, share a bathroom in the neighboring building with a serial killer. Florence: $8, no window, but an air vent next to a dumpster. Mexico City: $5, share hotel lobby with funeral parlor.

Just a few short years ago I was touring western Ireland with my buddy, Robert. After a week of sharing rooms with what I thought was a Homelite chainsaw cutting cords of wood all night, I was more than ready for a quiet night's sleep. Late one evening we arrived in Carna, a small Connemara village known for its Gaelic language school and unbeknownst to us, limited accommodations. We had two choices, a modern looking Motel 8 structure on the outskirts of town, or the Post Office, where a small sign advertised 'ROOMS'. When I inquired of the frail postmistress the cost of the rooms, she replied, "Six Euros, including breakfast." "Per person?", I asked. "No, per room," she said. "We'll take two rooms!," I immediately replied. Of course the mattresses were on the 'soft' side and the rooms a bit musty, but who could complain after a long overdue uninterrupted night's sleep. The fact that I spent two hours the next morning trying to get the ancient toilet to flush was incidental.

One of my more memorable rooms was in the Hotel Saint Merry in Paris, situated in the Les Halles district. Recommended to me by the well-heeled traveler Bruce Helander, this former presbytery dates back to the 1700's and actually has buttresses from the neighboring church protruding through the rooms. The catch was, the two rooms with a shared bath are a fraction of the cost of the normal rate. What Bruce forgot to mention was the fact that a metro station was being constructed just outside the front door. When I later told him about the early morning ruckus, he replied, "You don't go to Paris to lay around in bed all morning and for thirty dollars a night in Paris, what do you expect?" Good point.

Let me also say I've also had the good fortune to stay in some of best hotels, albeit in most instances on a client's nickel. My standard-size room at The Four Seasons in New York had more square footage than my house in Florida. The bathroom in my suite at Ashford Castle in County Mayo, Ireland reminded me of the grand parlor at Mar-A-Lago, except there was more gold leaf in the bathroom. My $600 per night Golf Villa at The Grand Cypress in Orlando had a jacuzzi the size of my swimming pool and the thread count on my sheets at The Grand Hotel Margitsziget in Budapest would have made Martha Stewart envious.

I'd like to think I've become much more discriminating in my older years when it comes to lodging, but as my friend Stephanie recently told me, "I'm not sleeping in any room that isn't as comfortable as my own bedroom." I've seen her bedroom, so I know why she prefers the Breakers Hotel when she comes to visit. For myself, sometimes a Comfort Inn will do just fine.

AT YOUR SERVICE

I usually had to listen to a long list of proverbs, courtesy of my father, each morning before school: "You get what you pay for; If it sounds too good to be true, it usually is; A penny saved is a penny earned; Do something right or don't do it at all; and finally; If someone won't stand behind their work or goods, don't buy it." Whenever I see the TV commercial that asks, "What can 'Brown' do for you?" I immediately say to myself, "They could have tried a little harder to find the package they lost..... and then they could have at least offered a refund on my shipping charges after they eventually did locate it, days later." Needless to say, I now use the shipping company with the new, shiny, yellow trucks instead.

Back in the days when U.S. car makers couldn't have cared less about quality, a friend of my father bought her first brand new Cadillac. From the moment she drove it off the lot, she immediately had problems. The lights and radio didn't work, at least at the same time. The windows leaked, the brakes made an ear-piercing noise and the key broke off in the ignition switch. This was long before the consumer had the protection of the 'Lemon Law', and the dealer refused to give her a refund or replace the car. My father, always one to help the underdog, made arrangements to have a local hauling company tow the car from upstate New York to Grosse Point, Michigan, where it was to be left in the driveway of General Motors CEO Roger Smith. When the dealer caught wind of my father's plan, he miraculously had a change of heart and accepted the return of the car and offered a complete refund. My dad's friend then went out and bought a Mercedes-Benz, which she happily drove trouble-free for the next twelve years.

For some reason, I'm always surprised when I receive service of any kind. But when I do, I always feel grateful. There are a few businesses that deserve recognition, because they offer a quality of service not often found anymore. For example, the local hardware stores: Hall, Sewell's, George's and Park Center. Go into any of these stores with an odd screw, bolt or spring. Chances are you will be immediately greeted by a knowledgeable person asking if you need any help. They will then spend as much time as it takes to find the part you are asking for, all the time answering any questions you may have, then you'll likely be charged less than 10 cents for the average fastener, a few cents more if it's stainless steel. I noticed a recent headline in the Palm Beach Post

Business Section: 'Home Depot Tries to Boost Service'. I say, "Good luck!" I'll stick to my tried and true, Shane or Bonnie at Park Center Hardware in Lake Park.

I find myself at our local Staples store several times each week, shipping packages or buying office supplies. Each time I am greeted by a familiar face, Cassandra Thorpe. She instinctively boots up the shipping computer for me, then places the required tools, a tape measure and packing tape that I more than likely forgot at home, on the counter for my use. Always with a smile, always asking if there is anything more she can do for me. That's the kind of service I can get used to, and will return for.

One afternoon I listened in while Breakers Hotel president Paul Leone spoke with a select group of employees who were being recognized for their outstanding service. He strongly emphasized how important service is to the hotel. "If a guest asks you for directions, don't point the way, offer to escort them. Once you've completed a task for a guest, always ask if there is anything more you can do, and always try to address the guests by their name." He continued on along the same lines, but I immediately got his point. There is more to a hotel than a nice room... guests there are paying a lot of money and expect to be treated accordingly. I guess they would otherwise would be staying at the Comfort Inn, where I didn't notice turn-down service during my last visit.

Not too long ago, I had a problem with the air-conditioner in my new Ford Explorer. It wasn't that it didn't work, it just made too much noise - a very irritating clinking sound every time the compressor engaged. I returned it to the dealer under warranty, and then subsequently made the rounds to almost every other Ford Dealership in Palm Beach County hoping someone could solve this annoying problem. It seems no mechanic could, and the last service manager summed up the situation up by telling me, "It does make a lot of noise, but unfortunately we can't replace it because it does otherwise work. Sorry." Not one to accept defeat, I wrote a letter to Ford CEO William Clay Ford explaining my problem and Fed-X'ed it to his attention at Ford Headquarters in Dearborn, Michigan. Two days later I received a call from Robin, who identified herself as Mr. Ford's executive assistant. She told me Mr. Ford received my letter and arrangements had been made at a local dealership to replace my entire air-conditioning system. When I returned to the dealership, the service manager looked at me and said, "You really must know somebody." Just in case, I kept Robin's phone number in the event I had any further problems down the road.

When my ancient cell phone ceased working last month, I called my provider, Sprint, and asked for a new phone. Being a customer for the past ten years, I thought I'd have some leverage. Of course I had to agree to another contract extension, but a new phone would be sent to me immediately. What they failed to tell me was that I had to layout $150, then wait 8 weeks for a refund. When I made an appearance at the local Sprint store to convey my dismay with this arrangement, the manager told me, "If you don't like it, go get your cell service somewhere else." When I relayed his message to the CEO of Sprint, Gary Forsee, I got a call from a Sprint district manager, apologizing for the way I was treated. A new cell phone arrived on my front stoop the next day, along with an invoice noting I was credited the $150 I had been charged for the replacement phone. Can you hear me now?

One of my longtime pleasures in Palm Beach is drinking fresh squeezed orange juice. Thankfully, Lauren, at the Tropical Fruit Shop knows just how I like it: medium size, with banana, coconut and papaya mixed in. When she sees me park on Royal Poinciana Way, that's her clue to get it started. Who said customer service is a thing of the past?

THE REALITY OF REALITY TV

Eighteen years ago I met with two English blokes from London in a scruffy hotel room somewhere in Pompano Beach, and may I add the hotel was nowhere near the beach. They described to me the concept they had to produce a TV series using real-life deputies from the Broward County Sheriff's Office. To say I was skeptical after hearing all this would have been an understatement. The bottom line was they needed a photographer to tag along and provide them with publicity stills and was I available to do this. As I looked around the tattered room with electronic gear and clothes scattered about, I thought to myself, "I don't stand a snowball's chance in hell of ever getting paid from these guys. And it's a stupid idea to boot." Well, as the saying goes, "The rest is history." The TV show they originated is 'COPS', one of the longest running, most syndicated and most successful TV Reality shows. Not only are those two guys I met, John Langley and Malcom Barbour, multi-millionaires, just about everyone else associated with that pilot season went on to have successful careers in Reality TV, except of course, me.

Just when everyone is complaining that Reality TV has sunk to new lows, I pipe up and say, "Have you watched 'The Amazing Race'? This Emmy award winning show pits 12 couples against one another as they navigate themselves around the globe. The winners, who must have the best overall time, rake in one million big ones. Of course there are a few death defying stunts thrown in, but a combination of mental and physical stamina will go a long way in this show. And for some reason I'm obsessed to becoming a participant, along with my son as my partner.

As expected, all the couples have certain 'dynamics' for the sake of TVdrama. Recently divorced, cousins (one being a dwarf), identical twins, gay and lesbian, dating, married for 40 years, father and daughter, high school best friends..... you get the picture. And I think I've got the perfect hook: Ex-hippie father/Democrat and Army Ranger son/Republican. Because of my son's advanced reconnaissance training, his navigation and map reading skills have to be a plus. When I mentioned my idea to him while he was home on Thanksgiving Leave, he told me, "I've never seen the show and I'm not interested." I then asked him if winning one million dollars was of any interest, and he replied, "I'll look into asking the Army if they would allow me the time off. It seems like it would be good publicity for the military."

I've always been one to cut to the chase, so when I noted that the show's creator and producer was Bertram Van Munster, a light went off. Bert was a fledgling cameraman back in the early days of 'COPS', and as luck would have it, he and I shared a horrifying and hopefully, bonding experience. Bert was riding in the front seat of the police cruiser, I was sitting in the back. The officer that night decided we needed a little adrenalin rush, so he turned on his siren and lights, and proceeded to speed towards a toll plaza in excess of 100 mph. I remember Bert screaming at the top of his lungs, and then recall him placing his camera between his face and the windshield, as a buffer I suppose. As for myself, I slumped down in the back, thankful I wouldn't take the full brunt of the collision between the car and concrete abutments lining the plaza. Of course nothing happened, but Bert was a little ticked off.

I am now debating whether or not to remind Bert of that 'moment' we shared as I try to prepare my application for 'The Amazing Race.' My wife rolls her eyes at me whenever I pontificate on what we'll do with the $1 million. Or actually, I'll be splitting that with my son, 60-40, in my favor. I also hate to put all my eggs in one basket, so I'm trying to come up with a back-up plan. 'Fear Factor', stomach is too sensitive; 'Survivor', don't play well with others; 'The Apprentice', hate wearing collared shirts and tie; 'Big Brother', agoraphobic; 'Biggest Loser', friends already tell me I'm the biggest loser. Maybe I should go the Game Show route instead. I'm thinking 'Jeopardy'. My wife often tells me, "You're a mister-know-it-all."

HIGH SCHOOL REUNION

Just in case you were wondering, I most likely won't be attending my 31st high school reunion this summer. I know this because I didn't attend the 30th last year, or the 25th, or the 15th, or the 10th or the 5th either. I did, however, attend an alumni mixer soon after graduating, which turned out to be a total disaster.

I had received an invitation in the mail from 'Cricket', class of '73, informing me that an informal gathering was to be held for alumni living in or near Manhattan. The venue was a Central Park West apartment with a large terrace overlooking Central Park. Since Cricket knew I was an aspiring photographer, she asked me to bring my camera so I could take photos for the alumni newsletter. The 'mixer' was primarily a mix of Wall Street, Madison Avenue and the Upper East Side, so my East Village attire (jeans, leather jacket, t-shirt and sneakers) didn't sit too well with the Brooks Brothers crowd. That aside, I found a few classmates who were willing to engage in superficial conversation, and then I left. The next day I received a phone call from the hostess, Missy ('72), who asked me if by chance I had mistakenly picked up the wrong camera. Apparently hers was missing. I asked where she had last seen it. "The bottom draw of the library desk," she replied. "So what you are asking me," I stated, "Is did I walk into your library, open the drawers in the desk, see the camera, and by mistake, pick it up thinking it was mine!" After a brief moment of silence, I heard Missy mumble, "Sort of." I thanked her for the invite, then told her, "Don't bother sending me any more." So much for school spirit.

Over the last three decades, my alumni newsletter has intermittently made it into my mailbox, and in each issue I notice that the class notes from my graduating class of 1974 are blatantly absent. There seems to be plenty of news from the class of '35 (Libby Atherson and her husband Fred have slowed down a bit now that they are 88 and 91. In July, they celebrated their 64th wedding anniversary......), but why my classmates have proven so uncommunicative, I can only wonder. I decided to contact the editor of the alumni newsletter, Mary Seymour, and see what her take on the class of '74 is. "I wouldn't presume to comment on the class of '74 in particular," she e-mailed me. "The 70's seemed to be a time when students in general didn't bond with their educational institution. Apparently, that sense of disconnection lingers for many." She also noted that she graduated high school in '76, so had first hand knowledge of this apathy. Mary was also kind enough to send me a list of 'notable' alumni, who included: Natalie Cole ('68) Laura Linney ('82) and Uma Thurman ('88). One person who jumped out at me on that list was William Morgan (class of 1893), the inventor of volleyball. Morgan would have been dismayed to have read the note that the parents of my best friend received from the phys-ed coach during his senior year: "Jon's failure to participate in the volleyball program has resulted in little or no physical growth this semester- Grade: F."

Almost everyone I've known who has attended a high school reunion has found the experience either completely wonderful or an absolute train wreck. Betsy Meany, wife of Lydian Bank president James Meany, is a Forest Hill High graduate who did attend her 10th year reunion, but has no plans to attend her upcoming 20th. "Honestly, everyone I know and care about I see anyway, so the reunion thing doesn't interest me. Then there is that pressure for the girls to go out and get some cosmetic surgery so they look good." Another local Forest Hill grad, Lucien Capehart officer manager Carrie Bradburn, made it to her 10th. She reflected, "It hasn't been that long, so it isn't as shocking as say a 20th year reunion". Bradburn opted to leave husband, Martin, at home, "So I could be a bad girl while he's home watching the kids." Palm Beach social dynamo Lori Stoll recently attended her 20th high school reunion, sans her husband Jon. "I went with my best friend and everyone commented that we looked the same. Unfortunately, the cute boys I remembered were now bald and the not so cute were now better looking. I can't wait for the 30th!" Art Dealer John Surovek never attended any of his high school reunions, "Because they tore the high school down sometime in the '70's." Surovek did arrange for a 20th year reunion of his 8th grade class, which was held in Hammond, Indiana, back in 1980. "I suppose there still might be a gathering of my high school classmates," Surovek told me, "But nobody knows where I am." Bruce Helander, who I once heard proclaim, "I'm not a reunion guy," is now planning to attend his 40th high school union this summer, in Great Bend, Kansas. Helander informed me, "Since I missed all the others, I thought this may be the only opportunity left for me to see my classmates, and besides, I'm curious."

For those with an insatiable desire to contact long lost classmates, the Internet offers 'Classmates.com'. Although I have never been tempted by hundreds of pop-up ads on my computer to register with the website, many have, including my old primary care physician. The Palm

Beach Post ran a story two years ago about a local M.D. who tracked down his old high school sweetheart through the Internet. After exchanging communications, they decided to meet, only to discover their passion for each had endured for decades. They decided to divorce their respective spouses and renew their romance, as husband and wife. What the doctor hadn't counted on, was an archaic law in South Carolina that prevented a man from 'stealing' another man's wife. My doctor was being sued for $1 million dollars by his new wife's ex-husband, and his medical practice was now in jeopardy. After reading the article, I thought, "Isn't it my luck, just when I find a doctor I like, something like this happens?"

I often heard my mother tell me around report card time, "I'm not so happy with your grades, but you do have some nice friends." Reunion or no reunion, I'm grateful for these friendships which have endured through the years. Maybe I'll go to my 50th ... after my extreme make-over...

WITHOUT A STITCH

Friday morning I looked out my window to see my two friends, Gary and Sue, pull into the driveway. They had boarded a red-eye flight from Seattle the night before, arrived in Miami at daybreak, then drove their rental car directly to my home in North Palm Beach. All this may not seem all that extraordinary, unless I tell you the last time I saw Gary and Sue in my driveway was 30 years ago, and they were sitting in the back seat of Joanie Parlman's Chevy Impala, both of them buck naked.

I first met Sue Rappleyea during my sophomore year in high school. She had transferred from our town's private parochial school, St. Mary's, which had closed due to a lack of funds and enrollment. Word on the street had it the students were also sick and tired of the nuns rapping their knuckles with rulers. As biology lab partners, Sue and I became quick friends. Our relationship blossomed, usually over dissecting some poor frozen mammal or pickled frog. After school or on weekends I would often find myself sitting with her parents in their kitchenette, listening to her father lament about Sue's boyfriends, many of whom, apparently, did not have the best of intentions for their daughter. Since I was in total agreement with them (and secretively had my own set of ideas about her), they immediately took a liking to me.

By the time high school graduation rolled around, I didn't have a clue for what I wanted to do with my life other than to never sit in a classroom again, but Sue had always expressed an interest in the teaching profession. Fortunately for her, she soon left our decaying, small, and depressing town for the State University of New York in Plattsburgh, to begin her studies.

We hadn't made arrangements to write each other, perhaps committing our correspondence to osmosis, but only a few weeks later, Sue called me to say she was home for the weekend. She was visiting her parents and wanted to stop by and see me. She also wanted me to meet her new 'friend', Gary. And there was also one other surprise. My old summer flame Joanie, who also attended the same University, was with them. I told her to stop by my house after dinner for a few beers. When the trio arrived that evening, it was unseasonably warm, so after a few brews I suggested we go for a dip at the swimming hole down the road to cool off. As was customary at the time, we all disrobed and jumped into the freezing stream. When we hurriedly climbed out of the water, I suggested we just drive back to my house without putting our clothes back on. Why?, I haven't a clue, but at the time it seemed reasonable. Sue and Gary were sitting in the back seat, I was riding shotgun. To this day I have a vivid recollection of getting out of the car and laying down on my front lawn, then waking up the next morning all alone, with only a towel covering me. Although I often thought about Sue, I never saw or spoke to her again, until July 2002.

Two years ago I was in Ft. Benning, Georgia, attending my son, Desmond's, graduation from Ranger Indoctrination Program Training. He had told me earlier in the day, "Dad, I have my choice to be stationed in Seattle, Savannah, or here in Columbus. I told them I want to go to Savannah." After the ceremony was over, he ran over to me and said, "I have 10 days to report to Ft. Lewis, in Seattle." I guess that was another lesson he had yet to learn.... the Army didn't care where he wanted to be stationed, they would decide. When he asked me if I knew anyone in Seattle, I remembered that I had heard through the grapevine that Sue had moved to Seattle. My old biology partner had achieved her goal and now taught elementary school. I told my son to call me from the road, "I'll see if I can track someone down for you."

When I got home I 'Googled' Sue's name, and sure enough there was a link to a Seattle School District website that listed her e-mail address. I immediately contacted her, informing her there was a person anxious to meet her, and could she forward me her phone number and address. I also stated it would be too difficult to recap the last three decades, but she'd get an earful soon enough.

A week later the phone rang, and the voice on the other end said, "Mike, I couldn't believe it....when your son arrived at our front door, I thought it was you standing there!" Our conversation continued, and the next day I received a series of e-mail photos of Sue and her husband, Gary (the very same Gary!) watching my son iron his uniform prior to his first day reporting at Ft. Lewis. I also learned Sue and Gary had an 18 year-old daughter, Ali, whose main interest was fashion design. Graciously, she was willing to spend two nights watching the 'Band of Brothers' DVD set with my son.

Desmond became quite comfortable with his new 'parents'. He was given a key to the house and proclaimed the downstairs TV room and guest bedroom as his own private quarters. Later, there was apparently a slight misunderstanding the night he showed up at 4 a.m. with a couple of cases of beer and 7 members of his squad, but Gary assured me afterwards that, "It all got worked out."

I had, of course, seen the photographs Sue had e-mailed me of herself and family, but when I, too, arrived on her doorstep on my first visit to Seattle, I couldn't believe how little she had changed after all these years. After our most recent visit to the Olympic Peninsula this past September, we all stood in the driveway saying our goodbyes. I insisted they come see us in Florida sometime soon. Sue's daughter was also about to leave for college in LA, and my son jokingly mentioned he'd be moving upstairs into her bedroom, "After I paint the room camo-green." She nervously chuckled, and replied, "That's the son my father never had."

As my friends were making their final preparations for their trip to Florida, they called to ask what clothes to bring. I told them, "This time, bring your bathing suits."

ABOUT THE AUTHOR

Michael I. Price was born and raised in Hudson, New York. He, his wife and young son moved to Palm Beach in 1985. There he began working for the Palm Beach Daily News as a staff photographer. Several years later he embarked on his career as a freelance photographer. His specialty became editorial environmental portraits, which appear regularly in both national and international publications. Today he divides his time between photography, writing and bicycle touring.